THIS BOOK BELONGS TO

_____

365 Days of Kindness for Kids

BroadStreet
KIDS

BroadStreet Publishing Group, LLC.
Savage, Minnesota, USA
Broadstreetpublishing.com

BroadStreet Kids is an imprint of BroadStreet Publishing Group, LLC.
Broadstreetpublishing.com

365 DAYS OF KINDNESS FOR KIDS

© 2021 by BroadStreet Publishing®

978-1-4245-6384-5
978-1-4245-6385-2 (eBook)

Devotional entries composed by Noemi Hedrick.

Design by Garborg Design Works | garborgdesign.com
Editorial services by Michelle Winger | literallyprecise.com

Printed in China.

21 22 23 24 25 26 27   7 6 5 4 3 2 1

Let love and kindness be the motivation behind all that you do.

1 CORINTHIANS 16:14 TPT

Introduction

It's not always easy to be nice to people especially when they are unkind to you, but God tells us to love everyone— even our enemies! You can be kind every day if you ask God to help you. When you spend time with him, you start to understand how much he loves you and that helps you love others better.

The devotions and Bible verses in this book will show you how important kindness is and give you some great ideas for spreading love, happiness, and hope. When you are kind, it shows others God's love for them, and there are a lot of people who really need to feel that right now.

Share a little kindness today and watch everything around you brighten with joy!

JANUARY

"However you wish to be treated by others is how you should treat everyone else."

Luke 6:31 TPT

Love Extension

> David said, "Is there still anyone left of the house of Saul, that I may show him kindness for Jonathan's sake?"
>
> 2 SAMUEL 9:1 NIV

Love is a gift that keeps on giving. David and Jonathan were best friends. They were always looking for ways to show that friendship. Showing kindness is one way we can tell people we love them. We will be there for them when they need us most. It builds trust. When you love people, you want to show love for the people in their lives as well.

Think of the person in your life that you love the most. Is there anyone they love that you are able to show kindness to? What about a friend of your friend? You can show kindness by doing something for someone you don't know that well today. It may feel uncomfortable to try something new, but God can help you. A little kindness goes a long way.

ACT OF KINDNESS

Make a new friend.

The Right Filter

Their purpose is to teach people
to live disciplined and successful lives,
to help them do what is right, just, and fair.

PROVERBS 1:3 NLT

Have you ever needed to make a decision between something right and something wrong? At first you didn't know what to do, but you chose what looked like the right thing. What happened? Did someone notice? It doesn't always get noticed and it may not feel great at first. It takes a great amount of strength to do what is right, but that doesn't always mean things will be fair.

Wisdom doesn't mean you always come out looking like the loser! Sometimes being fair means that you have to call someone else out on their lie and there may be consequences for telling the truth. The next time you run into a problem of this kind, ask God what is right, just, and fair. The best outcome is feeling good because you were confident that what you decided was right.

ACT OF KINDNESS

Stick up for a friend who is being picked on.

Bird Traps

If a bird sees a trap being set,
it knows to stay away.

PROVERBS 1:17 NLT

It does not matter if you are young or old, you have probably found yourself in tempting situations. You heard someone talking about someone else and moved in closer to the circle, and then added to the conversation. Or what about those times you turned to watching media to make yourself feel better? A lot of these mistakes seem harmless, but if they are not healthy for you or others, they could turn into a bad habit and you may regret them later.

Read the proverb above one more time. It is a warning. This proverb is simply about seeing the trap and avoiding it. It could be a person, a place, or a certain corner of your mind that leads you toward that trap you don't want to get stuck in. Learn those traps and be like the bird that stays away!

ACT OF KINDNESS

Look for a trap in your day and make a good decision.

Wailing Wisdom

Wisdom shouts in the streets.
She cries out in the public square.
She calls to the crowds along the main street,
to those gathered in front of the city gate.

PROVERBS 1:20-22 NLT

Do you think wisdom is hard to find? Do you know someone who is wise? Ever wonder how they got to be so wise? Wisdom is talked about as being a precious stone; it is compared to gold and silver. Wisdom in this proverb is like someone shouting in the streets. *Shouting!* It seems that wisdom might just be something you can walk by and clearly hear if you are willing to listen.

Maybe wisdom doesn't sound like a calm, soothing voice; it might even sound harsh. What is wisdom shouting to you today? Take some time to recognize what those words are and consider the reason why they might not be the words you want to hear. Wisdom doesn't always have to sound good but listening to its words will bring goodness to your situation.

ACT OF KINDNESS

Call someone you love and tell them you love them.

YOU and the camels

> After she had given him a drink, she said, "I'll draw water for your camels too, until they have had enough to drink." So she quickly emptied her jar into the trough, ran back to the well to draw more water, and drew enough for all his camels.
>
> GENESIS 24:19-20 NIV

When Rebekah walked to the well to get water, she did not know that day would change her life. Abraham's servant was sent to find a wife for Isaac, and he prayed that he would be shown who was right for Isaac from a simple act of kindness.

Not only did Rebekah give the servant a drink, but she also offered water for the camels. This kindness came from her heart not because she knew it would be rewarded later. Let kindness be your first intention whether you get an immediate reward or not.

ACT OF KINDNESS

Pour a drink for someone in your family today.

A Kind Risk

"Please swear to me by the Lord that you will show kindness to my family, because I have shown kindness to you. Give me a sure sign that you will spare the lives of my father and mother, my brothers and sisters, and all who belong to them—and that you will save us from death."

JOSHUA 2:12-13 NIV

This is one of the tricky situations in the Bible that may surprise you. Rahab hides Joshua and his men, and then tricks the authorities and sends them away by lying. How scary! It's almost like something out of a spy novel. She could have lost her life for doing it, but she knew she was a part of God's plan to keep Joshua and his men safe. She risked everything for them.

Sometimes acting in the interest of others feels like a risk. You might have to speak up for a friend and risk other kids getting mad at you. You might have to admit a mistake to a parent or friend and risk consequences. Kindness takes on many forms. Be brave and trust that God will protect you.

ACT OF KINDNESS

Tell a teacher or parent how great they are.

Loyalty

"The LORD bless you, my daughter,"
he replied. "This kindness is greater
than that which you showed earlier:
You have not run after the younger men,
whether rich or poor."

RUTH 3:10 NIV

Ruth was able to make choices about her life. She did not have to travel with Naomi back to her homeland; she could have chosen to stay at home in her own community. She didn't have to marry Boaz, but she chose goodness and helped Naomi over her own needs. In the end, she was blessed. Her loyal choices made her a woman of grace and dignity.

When you are faced with choices, it is only natural to think of yourself and what the different options will mean for you. In those times, remember to think about how your choices might affect those around you. You can influence for good and for bad. It is your choice. Choose wisely.

ACT OF KINDNESS

Say something kind to someone in your family.

STAND BY

Show kindness to the sons of Barzillai of Gilead and let them be among those who eat at your table. They stood by me when I fled from your brother Absalom.

1 KINGS 2:7 NIV

Standing beside someone who is afraid is an act of bravery that means a lot. There are many times when people are afraid. It could be they are dealing with a hard situation at home, sickness, or losing someone they love. You may have gone through one or more of these and could think of people who stood by you.

Think about what mattered to you in those moments. It was the people who listened to you, helped you, prayed for you, and held you when you felt like you had no strength. Ask the Lord to help you be that kind of person to someone else so they can trust you to stand by them no matter what happens.

ACT OF KINDNESS

Tell someone they matter to you.

Pay It Forward

> "May the LORD now show you kindness and faithfulness, and I too will show you the same favor because you have done this."
>
> 2 SAMUEL 2:6 NIV

There is a movie about paying goodness forward. It's a simple idea but would make a big difference if we all did it. When someone shows you kindness, instead of repaying them the kindness, you pass on the good deed to someone else. When they thank you for the good deed, just tell them to "pay it forward."

There are so many ways we can help others: simple acts like offering to take care of younger siblings, bringing some treats to the new neighbors, or helping your friend with homework. Ask the Lord to show you how to be a light to others by being like Christ in kindness and faithfulness.

ACT OF KINDNESS

Help make a meal.

Remember Kindness

When our ancestors were in Egypt,
they gave no thought to your miracles;
they did not remember your many kindnesses,
and they rebelled by the sea, the Red Sea.

PSALM 106:7 NIV

God worked some amazing miracles for the Israelites to show them his love, mercy, and faithfulness. As humans, we can easily forget the good things God has given us when we are in the middle of hard times.

You might be having a bad day right now. Maybe you are struggling with a sibling, or you are finding it hard to play with neighbors. When you have days like that, it is tempting to feel like God has forgotten you. Maybe you need to put the spotlight on yourself and ask if you have forgotten how good God has always been. Remember the good things he has done for you in this moment to help you through your troubles.

ACT OF KINDNESS

*Tell a friend or family member
what you like about them.*

Kind Of Hard

If a good person punished me, that would be kind. If he corrected me, that would be like perfumed oil on my head. I shouldn't refuse it. But I pray against those who do evil.

PSALM 141:5 NCV

Love can be hard. Relationships between people aren't always full of good emotions, laughs, and hugs. Sometimes we need to have hard conversations, and the truth we learn in those talks can be painful. When you love and trust someone with your whole heart, you can expect that they might point out some weaknesses or encourage you to act in a better way.

Good friends, teachers, and family members have a way of bringing out the goodness in your life. They will sharpen you and inspire you to be the best you. Instead of seeing their advice as bringing you down, try to see it as a kindness, or as this psalm says, perfume. Their correction is for your wellbeing, so don't refuse it.

ACT OF KINDNESS

Write a thank you note to someone who has given you good advice.

Loud and Proud

I will tell of the kindnesses of the LORD,
the deeds for which he is to be praised,
according to all the LORD has done for us—
yes, the many good things he has done for Israel,
according to his compassion and many kindnesses.

ISAIAH 63:7 NIV

God shows us his goodness in so many ways. Sometimes his goodness is obvious, like when you are praying for God to answer a prayer of healing for a sick loved one and then they get better. You might have been praying for a job for a parent and they got their dream job. But you can probably also see the goodness of God in smaller ways, and often these happen multiple times a day!

The wonderful thing about smaller kindnesses is that God uses people to be his hands and feet to spread love in a very real way. The next time you receive kindness directly from God or indirectly through others, stop and thank him. Speak it out loud, thank him for his goodness, and proudly share his care for you.

ACT OF KINDNESS

Write a kind word on sticky note and put it somewhere in the house.

The Mission

> The next day we landed at Sidon; and Julius, in kindness to Paul, allowed him to go to his friends so they might provide for his needs.
>
> ACTS 27:3 NIV

In your day-to-day life, you might not be able to see the big picture, but God is working in you and inviting you to be part of his perfect plan. As a believer of Jesus, you get to be part of his story. If you let that sink in, you might be able to see that the dishes you just washed, the phone call you made to your friend, or the kind sticky note you just finished is a part of God working his plan to bring Jesus into the lives of people around you.

In this Scripture, Julius, showing kindness to Paul, probably didn't realize that he was helping one of the greatest known missionaries. He is an unsung hero, and so might you be. Be encouraged that every act of kindness is part of God's mission through you.

ACT OF KINDNESS

Bring a snack to someone.

Growing Pains

He has been very kind and patient, waiting for you to change, but you think nothing of his kindness. Perhaps you do not understand that God is kind to you so you will change your hearts and lives.

ROMANS 2:4 NCV

When you were little, you may have been asked to wear a coat outside or to wait before crossing the road, and you didn't understand why. You may have complained and got frustrated, but a guardian held the rules because they know they were keeping you safe from harm.

You may have been going through something hard in your own life, either trying to break a bad habit, avoiding arguing with a friend, or simply dragging your feet at home. Instead of seeing your experience as unfair, see it as an opportunity to experience God's favor. He might be using this pain or boredom as an opportunity for you to grow and change. This is his kindness. Encourage someone else today by showing that you can rise to the challenge and face your battles with a sense of purpose.

ACT OF KINDNESS

Compliment the first person you talk to today.

comforters

Give praise to the God and Father of our Lord Jesus Christ! He is the Father who gives tender love. All comfort comes from him. He comforts us in all our troubles. Now we can comfort others when they are in trouble. We ourselves receive comfort from God.

2 CORINTHIANS 1:3-4 NIRV

On a cold winter morning, it feels good to be able to snuggle up under a warm, cozy blanket or put some soft slippers on your feet. We are comforted by the feeling of things that are soft and warm. In the same way, our words can give comfort to those who are hurting or feeling down. We can use warm and gentle words to soothe someone who is stressed or anxious or sad.

Our Father in heaven is a God of comfort. He will always be there to help us through our troubles. Look to him for those warm and gentle words and be someone who can pass that assurance on to others who need it.

ACT OF KINDNESS

Donate a few new stuffed animals to a local hospital.

DON't Withhold

We are not withholding our affection from you,
but you are withholding yours from us.

2 CORINTHIANS 6:12 NIV

Paul found out with his Corinthian friends that sometimes relationships can be painful. Sometimes, it feels like all of your kindness toward someone is given back. It feels one sided. It is difficult to open our hearts to others, but we know this is what Christ showed us.

Jesus knew what it felt like to be betrayed when he gave nothing but love. If you are feeling used or unappreciated for the kindness you have shown someone, remember that Christ is your source of encouragement and he is so proud of you. Don't stop loving even if you get nothing in return.

ACT OF KINDNESS

Help someone out with one of their chores.

Holy Goodness

> The Holy Spirit produces this kind of fruit in our lives: love, joy, peace, patience, kindness, goodness, faithfulness, gentleness, and self-control. There is no law against these things!
>
> GALATIANS 5:22-23 NLT

There is goodness in believers and unbelievers alike. People are able to love and care for others without even knowing Christ. But because you are a believer, you have another source to grow your love, joy, and peace. Think about a well but instead of drawing water, ask the Lord for strength that you can draw from him for patience, kindness, and goodness. You have a living example of faithfulness, gentleness, and self-control.

Rely on the Holy Spirit today and continue to produce the kind of fruit that only comes from Christ in you.

ACT OF KINDNESS

Be patient with someone today.

Not of Yourself

God's grace has saved you because of your faith in Christ. Your salvation doesn't come from anything you do. It is God's gift.

EPHESIANS 2:8 NIRV

We tend to be hard on ourselves. There are so many things on our to-do list. School work needs to be done, the room needs to be cleaned, toys need to be picked up, not to mention the extra jobs our parents ask us to do! We sometimes feel like doers, and this can become part of how we see our faith. Is it a checklist of do's and don'ts?

Take some time to read this verse over and over. It is not about anything that you do, or try to do, that earns you a place with God. You are loved and you are forgiven simply because you believe. Allow yourself to experience freedom from this truth and share the same kind of graciousness toward others.

ACT OF KINDNESS

Help clean up someone's room.

Dressed in Compassion

As God's chosen people, holy and dearly loved, clothe yourselves with compassion, kindness, humility, gentleness and patience.

COLOSSIANS 3:12 NIV

Getting dressed in the morning can take some effort. Sometimes we just don't want to get out of our comfortable sleepwear, we can't find the right thing to wear, or we just don't like the way the clothes look on us.

It can be the same way with compassion and other loving qualities. It takes effort and sometimes it feels uncomfortable to put on the kind of Christ-like love that the world desperately needs. A quick prayer or reading of the Bible just might be the encouragement you need to get yourself clothed with compassion for the day. Whether you feel like it or not, it looks beautiful on you.

ACT OF KINDNESS

Text a friend three things you like about them.

Paths of Peace

> Her ways are pleasant ways,
> and all her paths are peace.
>
> PROVERBS 3:17 NIV

This world needs people of peace. It is a breath of fresh air when you are in a troublesome situation and someone tries to calm the situation down with a soft tone and kind words.

Jesus was a person of peace. To pass on the gift of peace to others, we might have to lay down some of our rights in order to turn a sour situation into something sweet. The Holy Spirit is your helper in these moments, so rely on him to guide your words, thoughts, and actions toward a better outcome.

ACT OF KINDNESS

Tell someone they are beautiful.

490 Times

> Peter came to Jesus and asked, "Lord, when my fellow believer sins against me, how many times must I forgive him? Should I forgive him as many as seven times?" Jesus answered, "I tell you, you must forgive him more than seven times. You must forgive him even if he wrongs you seventy times seven."
>
> MATTHEW 18:21-22 NCV

If you are someone who likes to calculate numbers, then you would have come up with an answer to Peter's question as 490. This was not what Jesus was answering in response to the question.

We sometimes feel like we can be gracious, but we don't want to let someone take advantage of us. We think we need to put limits on our generosity. Jesus' response lets us know there are no limits on forgiveness, and it's easy to see why. The grace Jesus has for us, and others, is unlimited, and our grace should be the same. Get ready to forgive—over and over and over again!

ACT OF KINDNESS

Invite a friend over.

Into the Light

"I will keep you safe from your own people and also from the others. I am sending you to them to open their eyes so that they may turn away from darkness to the light, away from the power of Satan and to God. Then their sins can be forgiven, and they can have a place with those people who have been made holy by believing in me."

ACTS 26:17-18 NCV

Our kindness for others can go beyond a simple act. Having a heart for people to come to Christ means that you have to be able to see through the outside of a person. People come in all shapes and sizes; some are easy to like, and others are not so easy!

Ask God to give you his eyes for others so as you meet them, they feel accepted and loved. Spending time with people without a hard heart can be the very thing they need to draw them to the love of Christ. In this way, your kindness in accepting them for who they are will bring them out of the darkness and into the light.

ACT OF KINDNESS

Tell someone you are praying for them—and do!

When No One Helps

The first time I defended myself, no one helped me; everyone left me. May they be forgiven.

2 TIMOTHY 4:16 NCV

There are times when you can feel very alone. Maybe this verse is exactly what you have felt recently. You might have been involved in a family argument or lost a friend and you feel alone. Maybe you just needed someone to give you a ride somewhere and no one offered!

There are times in everyone's life where they have not felt loved. As this verse encourages, forgive those people who didn't show up or speak up for you when they needed to. And in turn, remember to be the person who does show up or speak up for others when they need it most. Show kindness by being there and not leaving.

ACT OF KINDNESS

Invite someone to sit with you for lunch.

secret sins

> People cannot see their own mistakes.
> Forgive me for my secret sins.
>
> PSALM 19:12 NCV

Have you ever been in an argument with someone, and it lasted for weeks, months, or even years? This kind of fighting can exist in relationships because we don't always see things from other people's point of view. We might say we have tried, but have you tried to step into their shoes with a heart of compassion and mercy?

As this verse says, you might simply need to think about that, sometimes people just don't see their own mistakes. And perhaps you are not seeing yours. Take responsibility for what you can control, which is to look into your heart for secret sins. When you start to look at yourself instead of blaming others, you might see how to stop fighting.

ACT OF KINDNESS

Make a card for a friend.

Listen and Act

> "Lord, please listen!
> Lord, please forgive us!
> Lord, hear our prayers!
> Take action for your own honor.
> Our God, please don't wait.
> Your city and your people belong to you."
>
> DANIEL 9:19 NIRV

Have you ever shown up to a party or a friend's house at the wrong time or even the wrong day? Maybe you left your homework at school or at home. There will be times when we fail. We won't always get things right.

This cry for God to listen and act should be how we pray. The next time you feel like you should be saying or doing something for someone else, listen to what the Holy Spirit might be telling you and then act.

ACT OF KINDNESS

Do a chore for someone in your house.

small Requests

> In my vision the locusts ate every green plant in sight. Then I said, "O Sovereign Lord, please forgive us or we will not survive, for Israel is so small."
>
> AMOS 7:2 NLT

The world can be a very unhappy place and you only have to watch a few minutes of news to see countries fighting, people abusing their power, and bad outcomes for hurting people.

It is right to call out for justice and to use your voice to stand up for those who do not have a voice. We don't want people who are already troubled to be even more discouraged. Pray to the Lord on behalf of those who might not be able to pray for themselves.

ACT OF KINDNESS

Drop off non-perishable items at your local food shelter.

compassion

You should forgive him and comfort him to keep him from having too much sadness and giving up completely. So I beg you to show that you love him.

2 Corinthians 2:7-8 NCV

Sometimes a person's sadness comes from their own sin or wrongdoing. You might know someone who has lost friends by being dishonest. Maybe someone has a broken relationship because they have been unkind.

We shouldn't wish that this person becomes sad or feels defeated. Just when it may seem like everyone is against them, you could be there to offer them compassion and show them the forgiveness Christ has shown you. Don't let this person give up!

ACT OF KINDNESS

Send an encouraging text to three different people.

Honeycomb

Kind words are like honey.
They are sweet to the spirit
and bring healing to the body.

PROVERBS 16:24 NIRV

It's too easy to see unpleasant words. Scroll through any well-known YouTuber's comments and you will find plenty of hate speech and people who intend to hurt with their words. In a world full of hurt, we can be different.

Use your words—whether written or spoken—to help others and bring light into their world. If someone looks nice, tell them. If someone feels down, find a way to help them smile. If you are visiting a sick friend, offer to pray for them. There are many ways your words can be as pleasant as a honeycomb.

ACT OF KINDNESS

Say, "I love you" to someone you love.

Enlightened

The unfolding of your words gives light;
it gives understanding to the simple.

PSALM 119:130 NIV

We are much more aware of the environment these days. We understand our role in helping to reduce waste and not pollute our air. It's what we might call being good stewards of the earth. There are other ways we can be good stewards of gifts we are given. God's Word is one of these gifts.

We have the precious Scriptures that give us understanding of God's love and how to treat other people. You can be an example of the words of Jesus. Study them, live them, and share them with others. Find a way to light someone's path today by helping them understand a simple truth. Let the Holy Spirit guide you.

ACT OF KINDNESS

*Write an encouraging message in chalk
on someone's driveway.*

simple sharing

> Christ didn't send me to baptize, but to preach the Good News—and not with clever speech, for fear that the cross of Christ would lose its power.
>
> 1 CORINTHIANS 1:17 NLT

Sharing the gospel isn't as easy as it sounds. You might really want others around you to hear the good news, but it's hard to know where to begin. If you have friends who don't know God, it seems weird to start talking about Jesus without any reason. It might help you to think about what the good news means to you.

Is it good news because you know that there is a God who loves you and wants to care for you? Is it good news because you know that Christ began healing your heart and he won't stop until it's finished? Is it good news because you know there is more to life than what you are living right now? It could be all of the above! If you can put some simple words to the good news, you might be able to share it.

ACT OF KINDNESS

Ask if you can Invite a neighbor over for dinner.

It's All Good

Everything God made is good,
and nothing should be refused
if it is accepted with thanks.

1 TIMOTHY 4:4 NCV

We tend to sort things in categories of good or bad. It's our nature to look at someone and, because of the way they look or behave, we might say they are bad. This is not the way Jesus looks at the world.

God created a good world: a good earth with good people. The next time you are tempted to judge someone because of how they dress, try to look at them from Christ's perspective. Don't be mean to them but try to see that they are broken. It doesn't mean you have to agree with their bad behavior; it just means you see their true worth as someone who is loved by God.

ACT OF KINDNESS

Thank your teacher.

FEBRUARY

We must not become tired of doing good.
We will receive our harvest of eternal life at
the right time if we do not give up.

GALATIANS 6:9 NCV

suffering but saved

This is why we work and try so hard.
It's because we have put our hope in the living God.
He is the Savior of all people.
Most of all, he is the Savior of those who believe.

1 Timothy 4:10 NIRV

The world we live in is always changing. We might have been hanging out with a friend one day, and then be told they are moving away. We might have had freedom to go to a movie one week, and then a pandemic hits, and we can't go anywhere. Life is unsettling if we expect it to stay the same. It is often said that the only thing that is sure is change!

If you are suffering this week because of troubles that you didn't expect, or because you are wondering why the world around you seems out of control, remember that we trust in a living God. He knows everything and he has made himself known to us, so we have hope in being saved from earthly sadness. Share that hope with those around you.

ACT OF KINDNESS

*Write out an encouraging Scripture
and leave it in someone's mailbox.*

Prisoners of Hope

> Return to your place of safety,
> you prisoners who still have hope.
> Even now I announce that I will give you back
> much more than you had before.
>
> ZECHARIAH 9:12 NIRV

You might feel like you are in some sort of prison right now. Perhaps you are stuck at home, with too many people telling you what you can't do, and it feels unfair. The feeling of being stuck comes in many forms. But what does it mean to be a prisoner of hope?

Sometimes the reason we are so miserable about being stuck is because we know there is better way. Let yourself dream of this freedom and hold onto the promise that God will give back the things you are missing out on. Let your hope shine so others can experience an optimistic outlook as well.

ACT OF KINDNESS

Smile at someone you don't know.

Aiming High

It is my prayer that your love may abound more and more, with knowledge and all discernment, so that you may approve what is excellent, and so be pure and blameless for the day of Christ.

PHILIPPIANS 1:9-10

These words might feel unreachable to you as you read through them. How can you be completely pure when you know that you are likely to mess up in some way today? Maybe even more than once!

Instead of worrying about fitting the description of what it means to be blameless, remember that Christ carries that burden for you. He has already said that you worthy of being in the family. He has made everyone who asks for forgiveness free from sin. Live in this truth and let your freedom from sin guide you into making decisions that are full of kindness toward others.

ACT OF KINDNESS

Make breakfast for someone.

courage

I expect and hope that I will not fail Christ in anything but that I will have the courage now, as always, to show the greatness of Christ in my life here on earth, whether I live or die.

PHILIPPIANS 1:20 NCV

The best kind of hope comes from those who are in the middle of something hard and are able to get through it with courage. You can probably think of someone in your life who has been through something tragic and still managed to battle on. Sometimes these people are more optimistic than others around them who are not suffering.

You might be one of the brave warriors that can talk like Paul does here. Let's be encouraged by the men and women of faith who have courageously walked the path before us and continue to show the greatness of Christ in our lives here on earth.

ACT OF KINDNESS

Draw something for a friend.

Shared Purpose

Does your life in Christ give you strength? Does his love comfort you? Do we share together in the spirit? Do you have mercy and kindness? If so, make me very happy by having the same thoughts, sharing the same love, and having one mind and purpose.

PHILIPPIANS 2:1-2 NCV

Many hands make light work. And even more than that, many hands with a shared purpose do even greater work. You aren't alone in trying to bring Christ's love into the world. There are many Christ followers around the world, and many who went generations before you to prepare the way.

Kindness and mercy are a shared purpose for all believers who want to see God's kingdom come on earth. Be strengthened in the purpose you share with others and use this strength to do something great today.

ACT OF KINDNESS

Text three friends, "Good morning!"

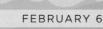

GOD'S PURPOSE

My dear friends, as you have always obeyed—not only in my presence, but now much more in my absence—continue to work out your salvation with fear and trembling, for it is God who works in you to will and to act in order to fulfill his good purpose.

PHILIPPIANS 2:12-13 NIV

A compassionate heart doesn't always come naturally. Some days we might be feeling generous or good natured, but at other times we are focused on ourselves and just don't feel like we can't be bothered to be kind.

In these times, encourage yourself with the truth of this verse: it is God who works in you! You don't have to fake the right emotions or come up with the energy to share love. Work it out with the Lord, tell him how you are feeling, and let him help you fulfill his good purpose.

ACT OF KINDNESS

The next time you go out to eat, compliment your server.

Interesting

> Everyone looks out for their own interests,
> not those of Jesus Christ.
>
> PHILIPPIANS 2:21 NIV

Even the Apostle Paul knew that everyone looks out for themselves. This is not something to be ashamed of; but it's something to be aware of. When you are considering whether to accept an invitation to a friend's house, or give your allowance for missions, or go the extra mile and volunteer at church, stop for a moment and think about what you are protecting the most.

Are you worried about losing your time or some of your hard-earned savings? Again, it's not wrong to think about yourself, but try to consider your interest and if you can serve Jesus by letting go of some of those things for the sake of someone else.

ACT OF KINDNESS

Clean someone's room.

Give It Back

Anyone who has been stealing must never steal again. Instead, they must work. They must do something useful with their own hands. Then they will have something to give to people in need.

EPHESIANS 4:28 NIRV

When children fight over a toy the argument usually ends with the words: "Give it back!" We don't like it when people take something that is ours. Ownership is a strange thing, and it isn't really what God's kingdom is all about.

Jesus said himself that he didn't have a home to rest in. He wasn't about trying to get stuff for himself. As our example of unconditional love, Jesus showed us a way that is very different to our world today. Try to let go of controlling your stuff and be willing to give to those in need.

ACT OF KINDNESS

Donate a bag of clothes to a thrift store.

Real Tears

> May those who sow in tears
> reap with shouts of joy.
>
> PSALM 126:5 NRSV

When was the last time you cried? Tears are an outward expression of the inward emotion you are feeling. Are you crying because you are frustrated or relieved on hearing good news? It could be a broken heart or empathizing with someone else's pain.

When we cry, we allow ourselves to feel the pain, or even joy, of the circumstances. It is good to be real about what is going on. If you are on a painful journey right now, or standing with a friend in pain, hold onto the promise of this verse that those tears will one day turn to shouts of joy.

ACT OF KINDNESS

Drop off a couple of Kleenex boxes at your local school.

DON'T GIVE UP

Let us not grow weary in doing what is right,
for we will reap at harvest time, if we do not give up.

GALATIANS 6:9 NRSV

You might not realize how much good you do in your day. Take some time to think about the things you do for other people. You might have a house full of family where you share in the cooking, cleaning, and house chores. You might be caring for a pet by walking it every day or calling an older relative to make sure they are ok.

These are good and wonderful things, so don't give up! God sees everything you do, and the world is a better place because of your giving. One day you will reap that harvest.

ACT OF KINDNESS

Put a shopping cart away for someone.

Restoration

My friends, if anyone is detected in a transgression,
you who have received the Spirit should restore
such a one in a spirit of gentleness.
Take care that you yourselves are not tempted.

GALATIANS 6:1 NRSV

There are a number of players in a courtroom. There are
lawyers, witnesses, clerks, the jury, and finally, the judge.
Everyone has their part to play, but the judge always has
the final say.

Friends, Jesus doesn't require us to be the judge in any
circumstance. God is the judge. When you see others doing
wrong, instead of calling out their actions or attitude, show
them mercy. Gentleness and help could guide them to make
better choices next time. Don't be tempted to join them in
their troubles; be the person who helps them turn away.

ACT OF KINDNESS

Send an encouraging text to a friend.

Built Together

Together, we are his house, built on the foundation of the apostles and the prophets. And the cornerstone is Christ Jesus himself.

EPHESIANS 2:20 NLT

While every home looks a little different, they all have foundations. As a believer, you have the same foundation of faith as other Christians. This is an important thing to remember when you meet believers who do church a little different than you do. It does no good to the world when Christians begin to fight among themselves.

If you find yourself fighting with other believers, take a step back and think about the things you share. Remember the teachings from Scriptures and recall that Jesus is the example for your thoughts and actions. Make every effort to bring peace to your brothers and sisters in faith.

ACT OF KINDNESS

Donate time or money to your church.

Love Beyond Measure

May you have power together with all the Lord's holy people to understand Christ's love. May you know how wide and long and high and deep it is. And may you know his love, even though it can't be known completely. Then you will be filled with everything God has for you.

EPHESIANS 3:18-19 NIRV

It might be hard to understand what you can't measure, but we can look for clues in nature. We can see the sky and the ocean, but we don't know where it ends. We stare at the stars and can't count them. This is the way we hope to understand the love that comes from Christ. It is something that can be seen, heard, and felt. But it is endless.

Think about that for a minute. Wonder about the huge love of God and use it to spill out into the lives of others.

ACT OF KINDNESS

Tell someone about God's love.

LOVE LOVE LOVE

> We love because
> he first loved us.
>
> 1 JOHN 4:19 NRSV

It's a wonderful cycle that is hard to break. You love God, he lives in you, you love him more, he lives in you more. We love because he is in us, and he is in us because we love him. You are perfectly loved by a perfect God.

In our relationships we don't always get love right. We show love when we feel loved, but if we are not feeling loved or cared for, we don't do anything in return. This is called love with conditions. We are called to be like Christ. Who do you need to show unconditional love to today? It could be your parent, sibling, or friend. Show Jesus to those nearest to your heart.

ACT OF KINDNESS

Show someone you love them by offering to do with them what they love.

Neighborly

Each of you must get rid of your lying.
Speak the truth to your neighbor.
We are all parts of one body.

EPHESIANS 4:25 NIRV

What kind of neighbors do you have? Hopefully you have the kind you like because they are kind and friendly. Unfortunately, this isn't always what we find living next door. You might have a grumpy old person or someone who talks meanly behind your back.

When we are trying to be like Christ, it means we have to try and see anyone, no matter who they are, like Jesus does. The next time you talk to your neighbor, remember to be a friend who always speaks truth and never lies because that is someone people can trust.

ACT OF KINDNESS

Bring in your neighbor's trash can.

FOR THE OCCASION

> Don't let any evil talk come out of your mouths. Say only what will help to build others up and meet their needs. Then what you say will help those who listen.
>
> EPHESIANS 4:29 NIRV

What was the last time you had to dress up? Was it a wedding, a costume party, or a sports event? Different occasions call for different styles of clothing, behaviors, and even conversations. It would be odd to dress in fancy clothes when you are at a big sports game, or to go to a wedding in rainboots. Just like you would think about what to wear before going to those places, so should you remember that wise words need care. Do you think before you speak?

The next time you are about to head out somewhere, take a moment to think about what situation you are going into and look for a chance to be an encouragement to someone.

ACT OF KINDNESS

Say something nice to a friend.

COPYCAT

> You are the children that God dearly loves.
> So follow his example.
>
> EPHESIANS 5:1 NIRV

Do you remember when you were young how irritating it was when a sibling or friend started copying everything you said and did? Our culture tells us to be unique and to speak our own truth. It can feel good to do things our own way. Yet this Scripture says almost the opposite. It says we are supposed to try and follow God's example. How? We try to walk in love just like Christ did. It would be impossible to do and say everything that Jesus did, but we can try.

Just like those times when you copied someone else, take some time to read and memorize the words and actions of Christ so you can be that kind of person to someone who needs it.

ACT OF KINDNESS

Don't be mean even when someone is mean to you.

parents

"Honor your father and mother." That is the first commandment that has a promise.

EPHESIANS 6:2 NIRV

Hopefully you have wonderful parents, but even wonderful parents make mistakes, and parents are hard to understand sometimes. It is still the job of every child to be honoring toward their parents, whether it is deserved or not. This might mean making extra effort to obey right away, cleaning up after dinner, or making a card to brighten their day.

Send up a prayer of gratitude for the parents you have. Forgive them for anything they have done to let you down. If you are struggling to forgive them, ask Jesus to help.

ACT OF KINDNESS

Tell your Dad, or a father figure in your life, what you love about him.

Sharpen the Edges

Suppose the blade of an ax is dull.
And its edge hasn't been sharpened.
Then more effort is needed to use it.
But skill will bring success.

ECCLESIASTES 10:10 NIRV

Making a cut with scissors that have a dull edge can be frustrating. Sometimes the cloth might tear or the paper folds with a messy cut. What a difference it makes when you have sharp scissors that give you a clean cut without a lot of effort.

This Scripture is saying the same thing but with an axe! Think of wisdom as that sharp edge. The more you use wisdom, the easier it is to choose to use it again. It will affect your decisions and attitudes. As you get better at becoming a more gracious and generous person, remember that you are sharpening the edges and marking your way toward a Jesus-shaped success.

ACT OF KINDNESS

Ask a friend or family member what they think about something and listen to their response.

Great Oaks

To all who mourn in Israel,
he will give a crown of beauty for ashes,
a joyous blessing instead of mourning,
festive praise instead of despair.
In their righteousness, they will be like great oaks
that the LORD has planted for his own glory.

ISAIAH 61:3 NLT

Mourning is the sadness linked to any kind of loss. This type of sadness looks different for everyone. You can mourn for yourself or others or even your nation. You might be experiencing loss over something you don't get to do anymore or know others who are going through a really hard time. You might even be concerned for the pain in the world.

In times of mourning, people can feel small and alone. God has a plan for all who mourn. He will restore their joy, and he will make them as strong as an oak tree. Allow your spirit to be lifted with this promise today and spread hope to the people you are mourning with.

ACT OF KINDNESS

Sit with someone who needs to talk.

Meeting Needs

The LORD is my shepherd.
He gives me everything I need.

PSALM 23:1 NIRV

Jesus is your good shepherd. He takes care of you and all your needs. Can you think of a time when you weren't sure if you were going to get what you needed, but somehow you got by? Jesus finds all kinds of ways to lead you through those times of need, including guiding others toward helping you. Think about how he also uses you to help others in their time of need.

You are a part of a bigger journey than your own, so find someone who needs help and give them a reason to celebrate the leading of Jesus.

ACT OF KINDNESS

Say something nice to someone at school.

Keeping Calm

Whenever the tormenting spirit from God troubled Saul, David would play the harp. Then Saul would feel better, and the tormenting spirit would go away.

1 Samuel 16:23 nlt

Saul had some pretty serious issues. Even today, we can see fear, anxiety, and stress around us. When we are experiencing times like this, we need to allow God to help us through and practice things that are good for the soul. It might be a long walk outside, a talk with a trusted friend, or hearing some music just like King Saul needed.

Today might be one of those days where you need to help someone who is facing a time of sadness or anxiety. Lift them up in prayer and ask God to bring them to a place of peace. With God's help, they can be restored to health again.

ACT OF KINDNESS

Text a friend and ask how you can pray for them today.

Made for It

> God has made us what we are. In Christ Jesus, God made us to do good works, which God planned in advance for us to live our lives doing.
>
> EPHESIANS 2:10 NCV

We don't have to do good works, we *get* to. God hasn't forced us to be anything beyond what he created us to be. What are the things that give you joy? Do you play music, have a good sense of humor, or know how to listen?

Use the things that come easily to you to help others. Good works may seem like hard work, but take the step and start doing what you love to do. You may find that the reward won't only be for those you are helping, but it will be for you as well.

ACT OF KINDNESS

Make someone laugh with a good joke.

Wasted Breath

Do not correct those
who make fun of wisdom,
or they will hate you.
But correct the wise,
and they will love you.

PROVERBS 9:8 NCV

Don't waste your breath! People like to get into arguments about all kinds of things. Politics, religion, schooling, sports. When you are most passionate about something, remember that it can be argued from a different side.

There is a source of truth in the Bible and this truth will always be full of wisdom. Think about what parts of an argument are simply opinion and what things are wisdom. When you give wisdom, do it with kindness.

ACT OF KINDNESS

Listen to someone's opinion without arguing.

Curse Reverse

"I say to you, love your enemy, bless the one who curses you, do something wonderful for the one who hates you, and respond to the very ones who persecute you by praying for them."

MATTHEW 5:44 TPT

Are you in a fight with someone right now? It might be an argument, or maybe it is more silent, and you are holding a grudge against someone for something they have done. People hurt each other; it is a sad reality. But we do have control over how we respond.

We can choose forgiveness. This is the only thing that can really set us free from angry feelings toward others. Try to put that person at the center of your thoughts today, choose to forgive them, and say a blessing. Pray for them, and if it is a relationship that needs healing, do something kind for them.

ACT OF KINDNESS

Pray for someone who has been mean to you.

NO SHOW

> "When you pray, don't be like the hypocrites who love to pray publicly on street corners and in the synagogues where everyone can see them. I tell you the truth, that is all the reward they will ever get."
>
> MATTHEW 6:5 NLT

Prayers are spoken to God and not others. You might have heard others pray in a group or a church setting, and they seem so good at it. But prayer is not a skill. It is talking with your Creator.

It doesn't matter how the words sound to other people; it matters what your heart is really saying, and it is only God who knows your heart. So, don't worry about every word being right; simply talk with God, tell him your needs, and share the needs of others.

ACT OF KINDNESS

Ask someone how you can pray for them today.

open Treasures

> Jesus, looking at the man, loved him and said, "There is one more thing you need to do. Go and sell everything you have, and give the money to the poor, and you will have treasure in heaven. Then come and follow me."
>
> MARK 10:21 NCV

The rich young ruler was doing everything right, but Jesus asked him to do one more thing. A simple task, but not an easy one. He needed to give everything he had to the poor. What a request! We might point the finger at the man and say that he was selfish, but what if Jesus asked you to do the same thing? It would be just as hard. It makes us wonder how generous we actually are.

Is there room in your heart to be more generous? It helps to set your eyes on heavenly treasures.

ACT OF KINDNESS

Give something you have to someone else.
Check with a parent first.

Quieted

"The Lord your God is with you.
He is the Mighty Warrior who saves.
He will take great delight in you.
In his love he will no longer punish you.
Instead, he will sing for joy because of you."

ZEPHANIAH 3:17 NIRV

When was the last time you turned everything off and sat in stillness? When was the last time you looked out the window during a car ride? So many things demand your attention: homework, practice, and helping around the house. If you can find a few minutes to be quiet, you might find yourself feeling much more peaceful. You might even find God in that space.

If you are able to find quiet time, let this verse soothe your soul. He rejoices over you, he is glad about you, and he sings with you. Let his love quiet your mind and heart.

ACT OF KINDNESS

*Go for a walk with one of your parents
(or an older friend you respect).*

MARCH

Be merciful as you endeavor to understand others, and be compassionate, showing kindness toward all. Be gentle and humble, unoffendable in your patience with others.

COLOSSIANS 3:12 TPT

Remember the Command

"Be very careful to keep the commandment and the law that Moses the servant of the LORD gave you: to love the LORD your God, to walk in obedience to him, to keep his commands, to hold fast to him and to serve him with all your heart and with all your soul."

JOSHUA 22:5 NIV

You might feel like you are always doing what other people tell you to do. You work at school and then again when you get home. You try to get good grades, but sometimes it feels like the list is never ending.

When you stop to think about it, you might feel like a servant for everyone else with little time for yourself. Be encouraged to look at your jobs differently today. You are playing your part in this world, and you are doing your best. In this way, you are serving God—the one who loves you and is forever gracious. Put your energy and best efforts toward your Creator. You won't be disappointed.

ACT OF KINDNESS

Write an encouraging note to someone.

small sparks

> LORD, you are like a shield that keeps me safe.
> You bring me honor. You help me win the battle.
>
> PSALM 3:3 NIRV

Sometimes we feel trapped, and everything seems to be going wrong. In these times, we need something that will help us lift our chins and keep going even when it is hard. This isn't about pretending you feel good when you don't; it is about letting yourself be encouraged with something you love. It might be reading a book, taking a walk outside, or listening to music.

In the same way, someone you know might need something to lift their spirit. Take some time to think about what they love and offer some practical encouragement.

ACT OF KINDNESS

Make a gift for someone who needs encouragement.

prayer chains

> God knows how often I pray for you. Day and night
> I bring you and your needs in prayer to God, whom I
> serve with all my heart by spreading the Good News
> about his Son.
>
> ROMANS 1:9 NLT

Prayer is powerful. You might have heard that from a
parent, preacher, or Sunday School teacher. But you might
not feel like prayer is powerful. You might have been
disappointed by times when you have prayed, and nothing
seemed to happen. Just because you didn't get the results
you wanted doesn't mean prayer isn't powerful.

Prayer brings you closer to Jesus because you begin to talk
with him. It opens your heart and shows that you need him.
It helps you think about others instead of always being
focused on yourself. Be encouraged today by praying for
others you know and feel the power of prayer changing
you from the inside.

ACT OF KINDNESS

*Text a friend and let them know you are
praying for them today.*

Good Reference

I ask you, my true partner, to help these two women, for they worked hard with me in telling others the Good News. They worked along with Clement and the rest of my co-workers, whose names are written in the Book of Life.

PHILIPPIANS 4:3 NLT

Sometimes it is hard to get a job. Part of the process of getting a job is to have people write references for you. You ask people you know to write about your skills and personality. Passing on a bad word about someone is too easy. We give in to gossip and we like to share our negative opinions with others who agree.

We need to be better at spreading good words about others. The next time you are asked about a person, find something good to say about them. Let kindness spread through the words you speak.

ACT OF KINDNESS

Send a thank you message to a friend.

Little Ones

Jesus called for the children, saying,
"Let the little children come to me.
Don't stop them, because the kingdom of God
belongs to people who are like these children."

LUKE 18:16 NCV

Children believe almost anything they are told, and they love unconditionally. This openness and innocence is what God cherishes about children, but it is also what puts them at risk. It's why we need to do our best to protect them from harm.

Take some time to think about how you can protect kids who are younger than you. These children need encouragement with positive and truthful words. Be kind and show them the heart of Jesus by keeping them protected.

ACT OF KINDNESS

Give a younger child a gentle hug.

Listen Carefully

> My child, pay attention to what I say.
> Listen carefully to my words.
>
> PROVERBS 4:20 NLT

There are a lot of mistakes made when we make a guess that isn't based on truth. Sometimes we make choices for others without asking them what they want. Sometimes we even talk about people without knowing all the facts. How can you avoid these kinds of mistakes? Getting to know someone helps us understand who they are.

When God speaks to us about something, we need to listen. It's important to listen to others when they are talking too. Put aside distractions and pay attention to the truth.

ACT OF KINDNESS

Put your phone away when you're spending time with a family member.

Signs of Restoration

> God said, "I am giving you a sign of my covenant with you and with all living creatures, for all generations to come. I have placed my rainbow in the clouds. It is the sign of my covenant with you and with all the earth."
>
> GENESIS 9:12-13 NLT

Spotting a rainbow in the sky is always a delight. The colors are stunning, creating a contrast to the simple blue sky behind. The rainbow is a sign of God's promise not to destroy the earth again. We are part of this promise and also part of God's plan for healing.

Make sure to take care of the earth around you so it can continue to delight us with its beauty and provide good food for us. Do something that shows you are as invested in this earth as Jesus is.

ACT OF KINDNESS

Plant something in a garden or help someone get rid of their weeds.

Those Who Serve

"Anyone who wants to serve me must follow me, because my servants must be where I am. And the Father will honor anyone who serves me."

JOHN 12:26 NLT

What do you think of when you hear about serving? Does it feel like something you are forced to do? Serving others is about helping them get something they need or want. Serving might look like bringing a meal to a new neighbor, helping a friend with homework, or getting younger kids breakfast.

Today could be the day to change your perspective on the hard work you put in. God is everywhere and wants to show himself to anyone he can. Follow him and let him work through you. Be a good servant and be thankful for those who serve you.

ACT OF KINDNESS

Say thank you to someone who serves you.

Looking Good

Suppose someone comes into your meeting dressed in fancy clothes and expensive jewelry, and another comes in who is poor and dressed in dirty clothes. If you give special attention and a good seat to the rich person, but you say to the poor one, "You can stand over there, or else sit on the floor"—well, doesn't this discrimination show that your judgments are guided by evil motives?

JAMES 2:2-4 NLT

We know we aren't supposed to judge a book by its cover, but so often we judge beauty on how people look. We think that success looks like someone in a fancy outfit.

It's not wrong to dress nicely for an occasion, but spend some time thinking about how often you judge others by what they wear. You know what it is like to feel like you don't look very good. Make an effort today to notice someone who might not be feeling great about their looks and give them some encouragement.

ACT OF KINDNESS

Say something nice about what someone is wearing.

I Enjoyed That

My mouth will speak wisdom,
and the meditation of my heart will be understanding.

PSALM 49:3 NIV

You may not be old enough to have your own account, but social media is a familiar way to share news on current events, shopping trends, recipes, and photos. Sometimes we see posts that really bother us and other times we see posts that stir our hearts, cause us to think, or make us laugh.

God doesn't hate these ways of communicating; he just doesn't like them to become too important in our lives. Instead of spending time scrolling through posts that make you feel good, choose to be with someone you love.

ACT OF KINDNESS

Spend quality time with a friend or family member.

Be Polite

> I want all of you to agree with one another.
> Be understanding. Love one another.
> Be kind and tender. Be humble.
>
> 1 Peter 3:8 NIRV

Simple words of kindness can go a long way. You can be generous with your toys or money, but this isn't any more meaningful than having a heart that is kind toward others. A humble mind means you don't think you are better than anyone else. It means you can try to understand others who are having a hard time. It might mean not getting mad when helping a younger sibling. It might mean being more of a team player. It could just be offering a smile to a stranger.

Being polite isn't about behavior; it's about our expression of value to others.

ACT OF KINDNESS

Hold a door open for someone.

Family Values

> If a believer fails to provide for their own relatives
> when they are in need, they have compromised their
> convictions of faith and need to be corrected, for they
> are living worse than the unbelievers.
>
> 1 TIMOTHY 5:8 TPT

Giving to charity, volunteering at church, and helping out at a mission are all very important ways of expressing our faith. God created the family unit, and he understands that your family isn't perfect. He knows that families are still an important part of who we are. They are also one of the best examples of unconditional love.

The bond that you have with your family should be treasured. If you are struggling with forgiveness for a relative, ask Christ to help you. One of the best ways you can mend a relationship is by offering a word of kindness or a hand to help. You might be surprised at how quickly a situation can turn when you prioritize your family.

ACT OF KINDNESS

Help a family member who is busy.

smile

When I smiled at them, they scarcely believed it;
the light of my face was precious to them.

JOB 29:24 NIV

Our faces can show a lot of emotion and let people know
without any words how we are feeling. Sometimes we
don't know the feelings we have inside our hearts. We
might be showing our displeasure or anger when we don't
mean to.

They say first impressions are important, which means
people can read whether you like them or not within a few
minutes of meeting. Sometimes even a few seconds. There
will be times when you pass a stranger, maybe a homeless
person, or a kid at school. You don't have words, but you
do have a smile which can be just as comforting. As you
think about the way your face is toward others, remember
that God's face is always encouraging. Picture his smile
toward you today.

ACT OF KINDNESS

Smile at three people you don't know.

Teachers and Preachers

Most of you shouldn't become teachers.
That's because you know that those of us who teach
will be held more accountable.

JAMES 3:1 NIRV

Nobody would argue that teachers have a hard job. Teachers in the Scriptures were those who taught about law, but it is true that even today's teachers have a lot that they have to take care of.

Teachers are gifted not only about a subject but in the way that they teach young people about how to treat people. They are often the ones kids look up to. Take some time to reflect on what it is like to be a teacher and pray that God would strengthen them and lift them up.

ACT OF KINDNESS

Bring extra school supplies to your local school.

Delivery

> He sent messengers on ahead, who went into a Samaritan village to get things ready for him.
>
> Luke 9:52 NIV

It's rare these days to get a letter from a friend or relative in the mail. Technology has replaced a lot of the need for that kind of communication. Someday robots may deliver our packages, but until then we rely on drivers to get the things that you need and want to your door.

In a similar way, there is nothing to replace somebody's physical presence. You might be talking with someone over text or social media, but when was the last time you set up a face-to-face conversation? Don't forget to stay in touch with people… nothing can replace a hug!

ACT OF KINDNESS

Leave a thank you note in your mailbox for the mail carrier.

Humbly Grateful

"When the LORD gives you in the evening meat to eat and in the morning bread to the full, because the LORD has heard your grumbling that you grumble against him—what are we? Your grumbling is not against us but against the LORD."

EXODUS 16:8 NCV

The way the Israelites acted seems silly when you read about all the complaining they did. Unfortunately, if we were to read a book about our lives, we might see the same pattern. It is our human nature to focus on the negative side of our situation. We want to grumble about our teacher telling us to do extra work, the friend who is mean sometimes, or the dinner we had to clean up.

You might not feel like these grumbles are against God, but when you complain, you are choosing to not be grateful for all the things he has given you. It's time to be thankful that you have a teacher, or that friend, and that you even had a meal to eat. Be humbly grateful not grumbly hateful!

ACT OF KINDNESS

Make today a no-complaining day.

Healing Gestures

Jesus went all over Galilee.
There he taught in the synagogues.
He preached the good news of God's kingdom.
He healed every illness and sickness the people had.

MATTHEW 4:23 NIRV

If you have ever spent time in the hospital or visited someone there, you will know how hard nurses work. When most of us are sleeping, nurses are awake, taking care of the sick. Nurses help people deal with their pain and comfort those who are afraid. Not everyone can be a nurse, but we can pay attention when people around us are hurting and be a comfort to them.

Jesus was able to bring healing for diseases and sickness and we can trust that he is still working alongside these faithful men and women to restore bodies, minds, and hearts.

ACT OF KINDNESS

Say thank you to a nurse.

Hidden Treasures

If you call out for insight
and raise your voice for understanding,
if you seek it like silver
and search for it as for hidden treasures,
then you will understand the fear of the LORD
and find the knowledge of God.

PROVERBS 2:3-5 ESV

Have you ever gone on a treasure hunt that was set up for you and your friends? Maybe you remember Easter Sunday when you went hunting for eggs! The thrill of finding something valuable keeps you motivated to keep looking until you recover it.

This is how God wants us to understand wisdom. The value of wisdom is more than anything we could ever dream of. Wisdom gives us a full life. It teaches the best way to live and how to get along with others. Search for this wisdom as a hidden treasure and get excited when you understand something more about the nature of God.

ACT OF KINDNESS

Tape coins around a playground for children to find.

Darkest Valleys

Even when I walk through the darkest valley,
I will not be afraid, for you are close beside me.
Your rod and your staff protect and comfort me.

PSALM 23:4 NLT

Valleys are a part of our journey of life. We need to walk through the valleys to get to greener pastures. If you are feeling low in your life right now, remember that your shepherd is near, and he will guide you through rough patches.

Allow yourself to dream about what is beyond the valley—fresher waters, calmer weather, greener pastures. Let this hope of what is on the other side make you stronger as you go. Take comfort in knowing that you have your Savior beside you all along the way.

ACT OF KINDNESS

Offer to clear someone's driveway or water their plants.

Remember

Rejoice with those who rejoice;
mourn with those who mourn.

ROMANS 12:15 NIV

In the first few days and weeks of losing a loved one, there is an amazing amount of support from the people closest to you. And while they don't forget, they do get on with their lives and slowly that support becomes less. You will never forget your loved one and it means a lot when others remember them too.

If you can think of someone who has lost a close friend or family member, whether it was recent or some time ago, support them in prayer and let them know you care.

ACT OF KINDNESS

Pray for someone who has lost a loved one.

Harmonious

Live in harmony with one another. Do not be proud, but be willing to associate with people of low position. Do not be conceited.

ROMANS 12:16 NIV

What does it make you feel like when someone else brags about how good they are or talks about their ideas as if they are the only right ones? This kind of attitude separates people. When one person puts themselves above others it is hard to want to be with them.

This is not the way of Christ. Jesus put the needs of people above his own. He sat with people who were rejected by their friends and family. Others decided that they were not worth talking to. Jesus was different. He showed us that all people are valuable. Hold this high value for others in your heart as you go into the world.

ACT OF KINDNESS

Say something nice to the first person you talk to today.

Put the Phone Down

Since we are surrounded by such a huge crowd of witnesses to the life of faith, let us strip off every weight that slows us down, especially the sin that so easily trips us up. And let us run with endurance the race God has set before us.

HEBREWS 12:1 NLT

It isn't fun to have your phone tell you how much time you have spent on the screen in a day or week because it is usually more than you think. It is a good reminder that we probably rely too much on our phones for all our information and entertainment.

While the phone itself isn't evil, it does weigh us down. We can get distracted and have a hard time listening to the people around us. You have so many valuable people in your life that need your attention and love. It might be harder to make the effort to call or meet up with them, but it will show that you care.

ACT OF KINDNESS

Put your phone away when you're spending time with a friend.

Pray for the Poor

Surely no one lays a hand on a broken man
when he cries for help in his distress.
Have I not wept for those in trouble?
Has not my soul grieved for the poor?

JOB 30:24-25 NIV

When our hearts hurt for those who are suffering, or when
we are sensitive to things that are not right, our hearts are
close to God's. There are a lot of hard things that break our
hearts. It is important to remember that Jesus cares about
our pain.

Broken homes, lack of food, abuse, and sickness are just
a few of the problems that our world faces. Instead of
getting sad about a hopeless situation, we can find hope
in the power of Jesus. Pray with hope, act with hope, and
spread hope to the world around you.

ACT OF KINDNESS

Pray for someone who is poor.

Best Medicine

There is a time to cry and a time to laugh.
There is a time to be sad and a time to dance.

ECCLESIASTES 3:4 NCV

There's proof that laughing helps your health. When you laugh, your body creates a response that causes you to relax. It helps your immune system, so laughing could actually fight sickness! Isn't it amazing how God created our minds and bodies to work together like this?

If you are feeling a little sad today, find some funny video clips, read a joke book, or think back to the last thing that made you laugh. If you get a chance, pass this onto someone else to help brighten their day.

ACT OF KINDNESS

Send a funny picture to a friend.

A King's Gratitude

As soon as I pray, you answer me;
you encourage me by giving me strength.
Every king in all the earth will thank you, LORD,
for all of them will hear your words.

PSALM 138:3-4 NLT

Writing is mostly done digitally these days which makes it easy to get your thoughts down. But there is something beautiful about using your hands to write the way scribes would have done for the kings.

A prayer might have been a much more thoughtful process because others would repeat the words. In the case of the psalms, words were written more like poems. Consider this psalm and how you would have written a prayer of thankfulness. What do you have to be thankful for in your life?

ACT OF KINDNESS

Write a thank-you note to someone in your house.

Night and Day

You know that I've been called to serve the God of my fathers with a clean conscience. Night and day I pray for you, thanking God for your life!

2 TIMOTHY 1:3 TPT

When someone is going through a really rough time, you may want to do something instead of just thinking about them. But you will know from your own experience that when someone tells you they are thinking of you, it means a lot. It makes us feel like we are not alone and that there are people who care.

This is the care that Jesus has for each and every one of his children, and he wants us to have his heart for others. The next time someone comes into your mind, stop and pray for them. Allow your prayers, day and night, to be consumed with care for others.

ACT OF KINDNESS

Text someone a "thinking about you" message.

Slow Speaking

My dearest brothers and sisters, take this to heart: Be quick to listen, but slow to speak.
And be slow to become angry.

JAMES 1:19 TPT

Arguments are never fun, and no one ever really wins. People are going to upset you, fight with you, or lie about things. But even if you are right, arguing does not usually help. It takes a lot of self-control, but if you can spend most of your time listening in an argument and hold your tongue for longer than you want to, you might just come away with a better understanding of the other person.

Try to understand someone's heart before you speak. Sometimes you do not even need to say anything; that can be a true gift to someone who needs to be heard.

ACT OF KINDNESS

Listen to a friend who needs to talk.

Family Fun

Miriam the prophetess, the sister of Aaron, took a tambourine in her hand, and all the women went out after her with tambourines and dancing.

EXODUS 15:20 ESV

Being with your family should be the safest place to be yourself. You can wear whatever you want, cry whenever you want, and be silly without worrying about their judgment. The scene this Scripture depicts is one of joy and unity. Celebrating with family can mean a whole lot of laughter. This is how God intended us to be toward one another.

We are created to love deeply and laugh loudly! If you are not close with your family, find some close friends who can become like family. Thank God for the gift of close friends.

ACT OF KINDNESS

Send a fun card to a close friend or family member.

Beware and Be Aware

A gossip betrays a confidence;
so avoid anyone who talks too much.

PROVERBS 20:19 NIV

We enjoy talking about others and sometimes we also enjoy talking badly about others. Sometimes we are just sharing with people, but we know when we say too much.

If you are in a conversation with someone who is constantly talking badly about people, remember that they are probably talking about you in the same way. We are all guilty of this, but let's take some action with our guilt and let Jesus help us choose our words wisely. Let's turn our insults into encouragement.

ACT OF KINDNESS

Stop negative talk. Say something positive instead.

Extravagant Generosity

She is known by her extravagant generosity to the poor,
for she always reaches out her hands to those in need.

PROVERBS 31:20 TPT

Wouldn't it be great to be known as someone who is always generous? It's good to be reminded that there are people who are far more needy than we are. It is okay to focus on the needs of our own families and friends, but this can stop us from looking around at those who are most in need.

Jesus was extravagantly generous, but it wasn't always about money. He gave his time, his attention, and his love to those who needed it most. Remember Zacchaeus—the one everyone loved to hate? Not only did Jesus talk with him, he also went home with him to have dinner! This is going the extra mile. Let's learn to walk and talk like Jesus and stretch ourselves beyond what is easy to do.

ACT OF KINDNESS

Donate some clothes to a thrift store.

Heavenly Inspiration

The heavens proclaim the glory of God.
The skies display his craftsmanship.
Day after day they continue to speak;
night after night they make him known.

PSALM 19:1-2 NLT

You can ignore God in your day-to-day activities, but you can stop from seeing his glory when you look at the stars, walk along the coast, or hike through the forest. Nature has a way of making us feel inspired. We see greatness, beauty, and wonder. We are aware that our creative God is so awesome!

If you are feeling uninspired today, give yourself some time to observe the true art of God. Go outside, read some poetry, or go to an art gallery. Let God speak to you as you smile at the creative world around you.

ACT OF KINDNESS

Post happy sticky notes around your home.

APRIL

The mind of the wise
makes their speech judicious,
and adds persuasiveness to their lips.
Pleasant words are like a honeycomb.
sweetness to the soul and health to the body.

PROVERBS 16:23-24 NRSV

The Living Word

All Scripture is inspired by God and is useful to teach us what is true and to make us realize what is wrong in our lives. It corrects us when we are wrong and teaches us to do what is right.

2 Timothy 3:16 NLT

The Bible isn't always easy to understand, but it is God's living Word. That means the Bible is just as real for you as it was for kids hundreds of years ago. Do you know how to read and live the commands of the Bible? The Holy Spirit is there to help make it clear.

You might need to read a modern English version, look online to understand the meaning behind certain verses, or ask a trusted friend what they think something in the Bible means.

Commit to read the Scripture. Pray for God to teach you and guide you on the right path. If you get some insight, try and share it because you are part of God's Word being alive!

ACT OF KINDNESS

Write out an encouraging Scripture and leave it on the fridge.

sprouting

"The kingdom of God is as if someone would scatter seed on the ground, and would sleep and rise night and day, and the seed would sprout and grow, he does not know how."

MARK 4:26-27 NRSV

Watching something grow is a wonder. We plant seeds, but we aren't really sure what is making them grow. Science can explain the amazing process of growth, but it's nothing that we do. We just wait for nature to take its course.

Jesus described God's kingdom like this. We don't have to worry about how things are going; we just need to trust that things are happening and be faithful to the Lord's work. He will take care of the sprouting and growth.

ACT OF KINDNESS

Help someone water their plants.

share My cross

Jesus summoned the crowd, along with his disciples, and had them gather around. And he said to them: "If you truly want to follow me, you should at once completely disown your own life. And you must be willing to share my cross and experience it as your own, as you continually surrender to my ways."

MARK 8:34 TPT

It is true that God has so many promises and good things for your life. There will also be times when being a Christian requires you to do hard things. You might have to take a stand for truth that means exposing a friend's lie. You might be left out at school because your friends know you won't gossip. You might even have a friend be disloyal to you because of what you believe.

Remember the words of Jesus: that you will share in his suffering. Be encouraged that this means you will also have him as a best friend! There will be joy as a result of surrender.

ACT OF KINDNESS

Make treats for a neighbor.

Christ in Me

My old self has been crucified with Christ.
It is no longer I who live, but Christ lives in me.
So I live in this earthly body by trusting in the
Son of God, who loved me and gave himself for me.

GALATIANS 2:20 NLT

How are you feeling about your body right now? You might be growing, and your body feels sore or awkward. That is okay. Your body is important, but not as much as Christ in you. Your body will change a lot over the next few years, but you can focus on your heart and your friendship with Christ.

When you accepted Christ as your Savior, you said no to sin and you started to live like Jesus. This new self is Christ leading you toward health, wholeness, and love for others. Thank Jesus for giving his life for you and find a way to show love to those around you.

ACT OF KINDNESS

Invite a friend to church.

Small Delights

> The believers met together in the Temple every day. They ate together in their homes, happy to share their food with joyful hearts.
>
> ACTS 2:46 NCV

School has become more than a place you go to learn. It's a place where the same people meet almost every day, and you will be sharing at least a few small things about your life here and there.

You probably also have closer friends in your class that you might have lunch with or hang out with after school. Sometimes this is where you get asked questions about your faith or your church. It can be hard to know how to answer but try to see school as a place to share the light of Christ.

ACT OF KINDNESS

Invite someone to sit with you at lunch.

simple minded

Don't be intimidated by those who are older than you; simply be the example they need to see by being faithful and true in all that you do. Speak the truth and live a life of purity and authentic love as you remain strong in your faith.

1 TIMOTHY 4:12 TPT

This world can feel heavy, sometimes it's good to have a way to lighten the burden. One of those ways could be to talk to trusted adults. Learn from their wisdom. Keep things simple and always speak the truth.

Let God heal your heart and think about his steady love in your situation and others lives. And then thank the Lord for the younger kids in your life and pray to be an example for them. Speak life and pray that they are protected with the joy of being a child.

ACT OF KINDNESS

Get some fun little toys at the dollar store and give them to kids you know.

The Greatest Gift

God has proved his love by giving us his greatest treasure, the gift of his Son. And since God freely offered him up as the sacrifice for us all, he certainly won't withhold from us anything else he has to give.

ROMANS 8:32 TPT

What is the best gift you have ever received? What is the best thing someone has done for you lately? The best gifts are the ones that make you feel like you are known and cherished. Someone has thought about what you want and didn't care how much it cost. They knew it would bring a smile to your face and it would be worth it. They were happy to give you something that would give you joy.

Jesus gave his life as a gift for you. He knew how much it would cost him, but his love for you was worth more than any price. His gift gave you freedom. He doesn't hold anything back from you, so enjoy his goodness toward you today.

ACT OF KINDNESS

Make a gift for someone who needs to smile.

unexpected Request

When Jesus came to the place, he looked up and said to him, "Zacchaeus, hurry and come down; for I must stay at your house today."

Luke 19:5 NRSV

Zacchaeus climbed that tree to see if he could find Jesus in the crowd. He did not expect Jesus would see him too. Instead of ignoring him, Jesus turned to him and said he wanted to be a guest at his house! Zacchaeus was surprised because he didn't deserve this honor. The crowd was shocked that Jesus was going to the home of a huge sinner.

Jesus extends this same kind of love and attention toward you. Be grateful for his kind response to you and pass that kindness onto someone around you who needs it the most.

ACT OF KINDNESS

Invite a friend over for dinner.

Free Service

As God's loving servants, you should live in complete
freedom, but never use your freedom as a cover-up
for evil. Recognize the value of every person and
continually show love to every believer. Live your lives
with great reverence and in holy awe of God.
Honor your rulers.

1 PETER 2:15-17 TPT

What is a servant? Is it a good thing or a bad thing to be?
Maybe we think of it as slavery, and we are sad that people
were forced to serve others. The kind of servants that
Jesus asks us to be done of our own choice. Paul called
himself a bondservant of Christ. That was someone who
chose to continue to serve their master even when they
had been freed.

You don't have to have to a life that serves others, but you
get to if you want to! Spend some time with Jesus and let
his love for you spill into your heart, so you have a desire to
give your time and energy to others.

ACT OF KINDNESS

Empty the dishwasher.

Who It Is For

> May he remember every gift you have given him
> and celebrate every sacrifice of love you have shown him.
>
> PSALM 20:3 TPT

Jesus is able to work through our lives. We are his hands and his feet. He doesn't need amazing talent, big words, or even years of wisdom and maturity. All Jesus needs from you is a pure and willing heart. When you notice someone in need or maybe someone who looks lost or sad, you can give them a kind smile. This shows Jesus' love. When you notice someone is hungry or needs a ride, you can ask your parents how you can help.

Every time you serve others and give of yourself, it is not just for that person, it is for Jesus. He recognizes your acts of kindness as a sacrifice of love for him.

ACT OF KINDNESS

Bring treats to a friend.

I Just Called to Say

Carry one another's heavy loads.
If you do, you will fulfill the law of Christ.

GALATIANS 6:2 ESV

Sharing your day with someone is one of the best ways to talk through the ups and downs of life. If you are blessed to have someone in your life who cares about your day, thank God for putting them in your life.

We were meant to live in community so we could share things. Other people can understand and support you or be a safe place to tell some of your ideas. That person is a gift! You can be a gift to someone as you share in their struggles and happiness as well.

ACT OF KINDNESS

Call someone you love and tell them you love them.

Mailing Joy

When the people heard the letter read out loud,
they were overjoyed and delighted
by its encouraging message.

ACTS 15:31 TPT

Letters were the most common way people talked long-distance in Bible times. People could be waiting months before hearing anything from loved ones. When the church received letters from the apostles, they were delighted to be encouraged from far away, knowing they were being prayed for every day.

Be encouraged that others are thinking and praying for you even though you might not have received that message yet. In the same way, be thoughtful about others and send a prayer their way. Even better, let them know you are thinking of them.

ACT OF KINDNESS

Write an encouraging note and send it to someone.

Who Is Wisdom

"What delight comes to the one
who follows God's ways!"

PSALM 1:1 TPT

We have a choice in how we live. We could choose to not believe; we could not follow the teachings of Christ. We could make up our own way. We could refuse, we could argue, we could fight. We could show our anger and throw a tantrum, giving in to our emotions and hurting those around us. But this is not God's way.

Do not go your own way and turn your back on the way that Jesus taught you to live. Choose love. Enjoy a life of delight by following God's ways!

ACT OF KINDNESS

Help your parents with the laundry.

ANCIENT YET PRESENT

Their purpose is to teach people wisdom and discipline, to help them understand the insights of the wise.

PROVERBS 1:2 NLT

There are many people we can learn from. Who are the people in your life that you go to when you need help figuring out the right answers to an important decision? Who is that one person you check in with when you know you might be stepping into something bad?

While people around you can be good and right sometimes, reading the Bible and talking to God is good and right all the time. Proverbs is a book that helps you understand truth, and, if you are brave enough, discipline! So, listen to its words that might bring you the answers you need at just the right time.

ACT OF KINDNESS

Ask an older person what it was like for them growing up and listen to their story.

Still Care

The LORD watches over the outsiders
who live in our land.
He takes good care of children
whose fathers have died.
He also takes good care of widows.
But he causes evil people to fail
in everything they do.

PSALM 146:9 NIRV

We can be unsure of people we don't know. There is something about strangers that makes us feel like we can laugh at their misfortune or not care about their struggles. In times like these, it helps to remember that Jesus cares for every single person, including that person across the street from you or in the car next to you.

Just because you don't know people, it doesn't mean they are not known and deeply loved by Jesus. Treat all strangers as valuable and try to love them like Jesus would.

ACT OF KINDNESS

Help someone load groceries into their car.

Rescue and Protect

The Lord says, "Now I will arise!
I will defend the poor, those who were plundered,
the oppressed, and the needy who groan for help.
I will arise to rescue and protect them!"

PSALM 12:5 TPT

When you think of a hero, do you think of someone who is able to fight off a villain, push someone out of the path of a moving vehicle, or rescue someone from drowning? Maybe you think of people who fight for justice and stand up for the weak. These are brave people for sure, but there are other ways of protecting your friends and family.

Sometimes we can be a protector by not saying harsh words about people we know or putting in a kind word when others are talking badly. We can also defend someone by showering them with positive words, so they don't think badly of themselves. See yourself as a hero when you speak life into those around you.

ACT OF KINDNESS

Post a compliment on the fridge for a family member.

Basket Baby

When she opened it, Pharaoh's daughter saw the baby. He was crying. She felt sorry for him. "This is one of the Hebrew babies," she said.

Exodus 2:6 NIRV

The story of Moses is a story of amazing kindness. The Hebrew baby boys were supposed to have been killed and Pharaoh's daughter would have known the rules very well. Instead of turning away from the child, she risked her position and possibly even her life, to save one baby. God had a plan, and the compassion of Pharaoh's daughter played an important part in the story. It's hard to not care about a helpless little baby.

Take a moment to think about the precious gift of life a new baby represents and pray for those who are at risk of harm or poverty. You might want to go one step further and give your time to help care for a baby.

ACT OF KINDNESS

Help a mom with a new baby.

Reaching Out

> The entire crowd eagerly tried to come near Jesus so they could touch him and be healed, because a tangible supernatural power emanated from him, healing all who came close to him.
>
> LUKE 6:19 ESV

Are you someone who likes getting a hug or would you rather people keep their distance? We all have different ways of expressing and receiving love, but it is important to understand that for some, a simple touch lets them know you care.

Jesus used a mixture of ways to help people: sometimes he touched them to heal them and other times he simply spoke the words. Ask Jesus to give you wisdom in how you might show you care for someone and reach out with a hug or a kind word.

ACT OF KINDNESS

Give someone in your family a shoulder massage.

Expressed in Nature

On the glorious splendor of your majesty,
and on your wondrous works, I will meditate.

PSALM 145:5 NLT

God created us to enjoy one another and the world around us. Take the time to look at the beauty of the earth around you. Ask God to open your eyes to how he might be showing himself to you. You might see his creative heart in the bright color of a flower or his wisdom in the way a tree is bearing fruit. You might even be able to sense his humor in the way a little puppy chases its own tail.

God's love, creativity, and power is shown all around you. Pray that God would open a friend's eyes to this truth as well.

ACT OF KINDNESS

Pick flowers for someone.

DOOR TO YOUR HEART

Make allowance for each other's faults, and forgive anyone who offends you. Remember, the Lord forgave you, so you must forgive others.

COLOSSIANS 3:13 NLT

There are times in life when you are deeply hurt by the actions or words of someone else. Letting those people back into your life might take time. Sometimes friendships end and God can give you peace about that. Other times, God may want the relationship mended so healing can take place.

If you feel like God is asking you to forgive a friend, you might need some help to open your heart back up. Jesus came to heal your heart, so you don't live full of hurt. Hand over your pain to him and allow him to guide you into the next step toward healing.

ACT OF KINDNESS

Hold a door open for someone.

JUST ASK

Be devoted to tenderly loving your fellow believers as members of one family. Try to outdo yourselves in respect and honor of one another.

ROMANS 12:10 TPT

Sometimes we just need to ask for help. Maybe you can't pick up all of your things at once, or you need a ride home from soccer practice. What do you usually do when faced with small problems? Do you make it harder for yourself by trying to do everything alone?

We were created to live in community; we need people to rely on. A good friend or neighbor is usually more than willing to help. You might even make someone feel better about themselves if you ask them for help. Play your part in the family of faith and ask someone to give you a hand.

ACT OF KINDNESS

Help someone carry something.

Earth Care

The earth is the LORD's, and everything in it.
The world and all its people belong to him.

PSALM 24:1 NLT

There are acts of kindness to people and there are acts of kindness to the earth. We might think of these as two different things but think about how much people need the earth. This world gives us our food to help us grow. We need the rain for water to drink and we need the trees for the air we breathe.

Take some time to think about how much nature means to you. Thank God for what he has made and know that it all belongs to him. Care for the earth as you would care for yourself.

ACT OF KINDNESS

Help someone water their garden.

Give or Want

Some give freely,
yet grow all the richer;
others withhold what is due,
and only suffer want.

PROVERBS 11:24 NRSV

It seems the more we get, the more we want. Often we think that if only we had more money, a nicer home, or a newer car, we might feel better. And we might. But it doesn't last for long. This is because we can't fill a God-shaped hole with other things.

Nothing in this life will satisfy you more than the love of Jesus. When you accept that as the only thing you really need, it will help you let go of the things you think will give you happiness. Ask the love of God to fill you now.

ACT OF KINDNESS

Drop off non-perishable items at a food shelter.

QuiCK WaLK DeeP TaLK

Training the body has some value.
But being godly has value in every way.
It promises help for the life you are now living
and the life to come.

1 TIMOTHY 4:8 NIRV

There's nothing like a quick walk to get your heart rate up and help you to clear your head. If you are headed outside, it can be a time to cut yourself off from all the distractions. You might be someone who likes to put something in your ears when you exercise or do chores—like music or audio books.

Try something different the next time you head outside. As this Scripture says, the exercise does benefit you but so will a great conversation with a close friend. Combine exercise with time to be with someone you love. Listen, talk, and help each other in your faith.

ACT OF KINDNESS

Go for a walk with a friend.

Eat and Drink

Whether you eat or drink, or whatever you do,
do everything for the glory of God.

1 CORINTHIANS 10:31 NRSV

What a relief it is to know that God created you to eat and drink as well as do all the other things in your life! God wants you to enjoy eating a good meal and drinking to satisfy your thirst.

Our culture puts a lot of focus on food, and we can turn it into a replacement for God. How? By living for food instead of for him. Allow Jesus to fill the space in your heart where you need him the most, and then keep doing all those normal things for his glory.

ACT OF KINDNESS

Invite someone to sit with you at lunch.

TO SERVE

"Even the Son of Man came not to be served but to serve, and to give his life as a ransom for many."

MARK 10:45 ESV

Have you ever met the child of a famous person, or had someone tell you how they know someone important? The title that Jesus held on earth, God's Son, was better than any title you will ever hear, but he came into the world through an ordinary family and grew up with a plain life. Jesus was not proud. He offered love, acceptance, and healing with a heart full of compassion.

Remember that Jesus is your example and your source of love for the people in your life. Don't expect to be served in life; expect to serve others.

ACT OF KINDNESS

Offer to wash your neighbor's car.

Culture of Help

Encourage one another and build one another up,
just as you are doing.

1 THESSALONIANS 5:11 ESV

There are dependent people and there are independent people. In our culture, we think that independence is the better way to be. As you get older, you might think you should first try to do things by yourself before asking for help. Unfortunately, this might mean missing out on spending time with someone or struggling alone and getting frustrated when you don't need to.

It is good to ask for help. People feel useful when they have the opportunity to use their gifts. You never know when your help will be asked for in return.

ACT OF KINDNESS

Offer to do the dishes tonight.

I'd Rather Not

"The greatest among you must be a servant."

MATTHEW 23:11 NLT

Doing well in school usually happens by getting good grades on tests and assignments. This doesn't always show how well people can actually work. It doesn't seem right that those who brag about their work often get noticed. Jesus turned this thinking upside down by showing that becoming a servant and being humble is the best way to be.

Even though this way of thinking doesn't always win at school, a teacher will probably notice your kindness and willingness to serve more than you realize. And even if it is never rewarded, it is noticed in God's kingdom.

ACT OF KINDNESS

Pour someone a drink.

Unmerited

> Servants, be subject to your masters with all respect, not only to the good and gentle but also to the unjust.
>
> 1 PETER 2:18 ESV

Being a leader can be lonely. Whether a teacher is fair or not, they are different from the students. They have authority and they make decisions. This means that often they will get talked about behind their backs.

Jesus showed us that everyone needs to be respected. Be a part of changing the culture in your classroom and show respect toward the person who is in charge.

ACT OF KINDNESS

Help clear the table.

Cheerful Face

A happy heart makes the face cheerful,
but heartache crushes the spirit.

PROVERBS 15:13 NIV

Our face shows what our heart is feeling. When we feel good inside, our faces are usually relaxed and quick to smile. When we are worried, our expressions are tense. You might need to think of something you are thankful for, and then send a prayer of thanksgiving to God. You might need to get outside for a moment to clear your head. You might just need to take a couple of really deep breaths.

Ask Jesus to give you the tools you need to lift your spirits, so your face can be cheerful and light. You don't have to be fake about your feelings; be real and let God lead you into a place of joy.

ACT OF KINDNESS

Smile at three people you don't know today.

MAY

Whoever pursues righteousness
and kindness will find life,
righteousness, and honor.

PROVERBS 21:21 ESV

Watch and Learn

"Look at all the birds—do you think they worry about their existence? They don't plant or reap or store up food, yet your heavenly Father provides them each with food. Aren't you much more valuable to your Father than they?"

MATTHEW 6:26 TPT

If you are ever outside in a public area, you will see birds hanging around. They are on the lookout for food for themselves or to bring to their young. Birds have an amazing way of finding what they need, and they rarely starve. Think about the way these birds are provided for. Their food source is mostly out of their control; they just have to be ready to go and find it!

You might be worried about your parents or someone else right now. You might be lonely or worried about someone who is sick. You are so valuable to your Father in heaven. Ask him to help and then listen as he points you in the right direction.

ACT OF KINDNESS

Feed the birds.

Despair to Wear

I am overwhelmed with joy in the Lord my God!
For he has dressed me with the clothing of salvation
and draped me in a robe of righteousness.
I am like a bridegroom dressed for his wedding
or a bride with her jewels.

Isaiah 61:10 TPT

Sometimes we think too much about what we wear and what we look like. The world tells us ideas through social media that make us think we need to look a certain way to be loved. Instead of being content with our own beauty, we compare ourselves to others.

You are so much more than just your outward appearance. You have a body, a spirit, and a soul. God says you are beautiful, and his voice matters the most. You have such a rich inheritance as a child of the King. You are dressed in clothes of righteousness, and they look stunning on you!

ACT OF KINDNESS

Drop off a bag of gently used items at a thrift store.

Model Teacher

> Show yourself in all respects to be a model of good works, and in your teaching show integrity, dignity, and sound speech that cannot be condemned, so that an opponent may be put to shame, having nothing evil to say about us.
>
> TITUS 2:7-8 ESV

Do you remember the name of your favorite teacher? What was it about them that you liked? Perhaps they were really good at explaining things or they took time to help you when you were struggling. Maybe they were really kind and made you feel good about learning. These kinds of teachers are great role models. They help us understand what integrity, dignity, and kindness look like.

God has blessed teachers, but with that role comes great responsibility. Pray for the teachers you know in your life. Pray for those who are tired or for those who are learning to be teachers. Encourage them and thank them for doing a great job.

ACT OF KINDNESS

Say thank you to a teacher.

Friend count

> A person with unfaithful friends soon comes to ruin.
> But there is a friend who sticks closer than a brother.
>
> PROVERBS 18:24 NIRV

Do you have a lot of friends? How many of these friends do you actually see on a weekly basis? There's nothing wrong with having friends on social media, but just remember these are not the people who should have the greatest impact on your life. You don't need to prove your value to people who don't know you.

There is a difference between people you know and true friends. Think about the friends in your life who you can rely on when things are hard. Think about those who text or call you often to check on you. These are your true friends and the ones you should invest your time in. Be kind to your contacts but be loyal to your true friends.

ACT OF KINDNESS

Text a kind word to a friend.

Seeing Clearly

> The precepts of the LORD are right,
> giving joy to the heart.
> The commands of the LORD are radiant,
> giving light to the eyes.
>
> PSALM 19:8 NIV

You might have to get glasses someday when things look fuzzy or out of focus. At times, our spiritual life needs this same kind of attention. When we can't see well, we need to turn a light on.

Turning to God brings things back into focus again. The world will appear brighter and clearer, just like when you put on a new pair of glasses. We don't always have trouble seeing because of sin, sometimes it's just the world around us that demands so much attention we begin to lose our focus. Ask God to help you see more clearly today.

ACT OF KINDNESS

Give some new or gently used books to a teacher.

DON'T WASTE IT

When they had all had enough to eat,
he said to his disciples,
"Gather the pieces that are left over.
Let nothing be wasted."

JOHN 6:12 NIV

It is not a new idea to limit how much you waste. We have become a society that uses so much, and we have not done very well thinking about what we leave behind. Jesus had a heart for making sure nothing went to waste.

We should think carefully about what to do with our waste. It might be that it can somehow be reduced, recycled, or reused. Make a little effort, and in the words of Jesus, "Let nothing be wasted!"

ACT OF KINDNESS

Go for a walk and pick up trash around your neighborhood. Make sure you wear gloves!

Given and Gifted

> "Give, and it will be given to you.
> A good measure, pressed down,
> shaken together and running over,
> will be poured into your lap.
> For with the measure you use,
> it will be measured to you."
>
> LUKE 6:38 NIV

Making wine starts by squishing grapes until the juice comes out of them. As you can imagine, the more you stomp, the more juice comes out, and the more room you make to put more grapes in.

When you share your heart with someone, it might feel a bit like you are being squeezed. It's hard to give extra money when you don't have much of it yourself, and it's hard to show gratitude to someone who has been unkind to you. Giving can be hard! But the more you give, the more you are going to produce goodness in your life and in the lives of others. Giving makes room for more.

ACT OF KINDNESS

Give your allowance to missions.

Grand Gestures

Love completes the laws of God.
All of the law can be summarized in one grand
statement: "Demonstrate love to your neighbor,
even as you care for and love yourself."

GALATIANS 5:14 TPT

Do you feel tired when you think about all the things you need to get done? Maybe at the end of the day you just don't want to do one more thing. It's likely that there are others around you who feel the same.

Take a moment to think about your neighbor's day. Are they young parents who need some time alone? Is it an elderly person who might be feeling a little lonely? There will be different needs depending on who lives around you, and you might not even want to think about others right now! Jesus might want you to offer some of your time today. If you do, he will give you the strength you need and there will be a reward.

ACT OF KINDNESS

Offer to walk a neighbor's dog.

Self-Seeking

For those who are self-seeking
and do not obey the truth,
but obey unrighteousness,
there will be wrath and fury.

ROMANS 2:8 ESV

It's easy to be comfortable with our own opinions, situations, and emotions. While it's not wrong to be caught up in what is going on, it doesn't help when all we can think about is how things affect us personally. What kind of situation are you in at the moment? Are you holding onto an old hurt? Are you in the process of making an important decision? Is there a friend you are really struggling with?

Take a moment to t try to understand the situation from someone else's point of view. You don't have to agree with them, but you can think of what a teacher or grandparent might say instead. Even better, think about what Jesus would be hoping for in the situation. Step back for a moment and let grace win.

ACT OF KINDNESS

Let someone else choose what to watch.

HOMES AND HEARTS

My people will live free from worry
in secure, quiet homes of peace.

ISAIAH 32:18 TPT

Have you ever heard the saying, "Home is where the heart is"? If we put enough heart into the place we live, we can make it feel more like home. You might not be enjoying your house at the moment for one reason or another.

In the times you are sad about your home life, remember this verse. God says that his people will live free from worry in secure and quiet homes of peace. While you might not be feeling that way about your situation, spend some time being thankful about what you do enjoy about your house. Start to invest a little of your heart into the people you live with and allow God to change your attitude.

ACT OF KINDNESS

Make someone in your house breakfast.

Entertaining Angels

Do not neglect to show hospitality to strangers, for thereby some have entertained angels unawares.

HEBREWS 13:2 ESV

Do you think of yourself as a welcoming person, or do you see that as someone else's gift? There are many people who seem to be so good at inviting people over and making them feel like they are special.

Serving others is about a heart attitude. It is being willing to put yourself out there for the sake of someone else. You never know when these moments will come. You might have a neighbor ask to borrow a cup of flour, or you might see a mother struggling to get groceries out of her car and hold her baby at the same time. You can show hospitality in these moments! And you never know who you might be helping. Strangers are God's precious children too.

ACT OF KINDNESS

Wash someone else's dishes for them today.

PEACE TO THIS HOUSE

"When you enter a house,
first say, 'Peace to this house.'"

LUKE 10:5 NIV

It might be odd to say this verse when you go into someone's home, but you can try it in your own words or even with your actions. The next time you are invited to someone's house, send a simple prayer to Jesus asking him to keep the home safe and comfortable. Take time to notice things and compliment someone on how nice something in their home is.

Make people feel at ease by being helpful and courteous, rather than creating stress. Be aware of the words you use and make sure they are kind. Be like Jesus and make people feel good in their own space.

ACT OF KINDNESS

Tell someone how lovely their home looks.

Generosity

The house of the righteous contains great treasure,
but the income of the wicked brings ruin.

PROVERBS 15:6 NIV

We can hold onto our stuff a little too tightly. We work hard, but it is easy to keep all of that money for yourself. Sometimes we might need a gentle reminder that it is God who has given us the ability to work or earn. He has made sure to provide for us.

Don't fall into the way of the wicked and hold onto your money so tightly that you forget to use it for good. Ask God to show you ways you can be generous and spread his love even further than your immediate family. Let him shine through your actions to others.

ACT OF KINDNESS

Load the dishes into the dishwasher.

confessions

Confess your sins to each other and pray for
each other so that you may be healed.
The earnest prayer of a righteous person has
great power and produces wonderful results.

JAMES 5:16 NLT

There can be a lot of tension in a home. Sometimes it is
because we are tired or annoyed and it can cause little
outbursts. You might not like the way someone loaded the
dishwasher, or you might be upset that they didn't even try
to clean up. You might have made a snarky comment that
triggered someone to overreact and now you aren't talking
anymore.

There are times when issues can run a lot deeper and
require some working through. You might need help and
time for healing to take place. Make sure to offer as much
grace as you can in your home. Tell your family when you
have been too angry or too sensitive. Deal with sin straight
away so it doesn't go deeper. Do things to make people
smile and show love in small ways.

ACT OF KINDNESS

Write a thank-you note to someone in your house.

It Will Be Okay

We know that in all things God works
for the good of those who love him.
He appointed them to be saved
in keeping with his purpose.

ROMANS 8:28 NIRV

There are many things in life that shake us. When the people you love lose jobs, get divorced, become very sick, or die, you know it will take a while to feel okay again. If you have gone through any of these extreme things, you know how important it is to have people around you encourage you. You need someone to tell you that it is going to be okay.

Thankfully, God's Word does tell us it is going to be okay. The journey might be rough, but in the end, God knows your pain, and he cares deeply about helping restore your life. If you turn your face to him, he will show you that he can work everything together for good. Remember to be the friend who encourages people with hope in their times of pain.

ACT OF KINDNESS

Write an encouraging note to someone.

Shiny New Things

"Strive first for the kingdom of God
and his righteousness, and all
these things will be given to
you as well."

MATTHEW 6:33 NRSV

We love shiny new things. It's not long before a new device becomes last year's news, and the bigger and better thing is out. We think we will love the shiny new thing and having it will make us feel fulfilled. But this feeling is fleeting, which means it goes as quickly as it came, and we are soon wanting the next best thing.

This verse is important to keep at the top of your mind and heart. Seek God and his kingdom first. Knowing God and understanding his purpose will make you feel much more at peace than that shiny new thing. Be part of his plan to bring joy and healing to others.

ACT OF KINDNESS

Bring toys to a homeless shelter.

wounds

> He heals the brokenhearted
> and bandages their wounds.
>
> PSALM 147:3 NCV

Do you remember the last time you were in so much pain it made you cry? As a child, tears come quickly every time you get hurt. As you get older, you learn to control those tears and let out a few words of anger instead. There are some pains that don't go away quickly, and they might leave you feeling down.

In these times, remember that God knows and cares about how you are feeling. He wants to bring healing to you. We don't always get the instant healing we ask for, but we can still ask, believe, and hope for it. Be thankful that one day all pain will be gone for good, and God will give back the years we lost.

ACT OF KINDNESS

Drop off coloring books at a children's hospital.

Sweet Tooth

My child, eat honey, for it is good,
and the honeycomb is sweet to the taste.
In the same way, wisdom is sweet to your soul.
If you find it, you will have a bright future,
and your hopes will not be cut short.

PROVERBS 24:13-14 NLT

There isn't much that compares to a cookie with a glass of milk. We love our sweets, and we talk about them as treats. Sweet food is as pleasant as wisdom according to this Bible verse. It's not just knowledge that is good, but it is true understanding that encourages people and helps them to smile or even laugh.

The next time you are chatting with a friend, try to hear wisdom from what they have to say. If they are struggling, encourage them with the wise words of Scripture. Find good things to talk about that encourage the sweetness of wisdom.

ACT OF KINDNESS

Bake cookies for a friend.

Read and Learn

To these four young men God gave
knowledge and understanding of
all kinds of literature and learning.
And Daniel could understand visions
and dreams of all kinds.

DANIEL 1:17 NIV

It is often said that the best thing you can do for your education is to learn to enjoy reading. You might think that reading is not really your thing, or you might have grown up reading a lot. It's not about whether you are good at reading or not, it's about whether you can find the kind of book that will keep you interested.

Daniel was a young man who loved God very much. When he was given books to learn about God and his creation, he read them a lot. He became so knowledgeable that he could understand all kinds of visions and dreams. Find a topic that makes you feel alive when you read about it and start the journey of learning.

ACT OF KINDNESS

Read your favorite book to someone.

faith and works

A person's body without their spirit is dead.
In the same way, faith without good deeds is dead.

JAMES 2:26 NIRV

A body is no less a body when there isn't a spirit, but it doesn't truly represent who a person is unless they are breathing, moving, and speaking. In the same way, our faith is still faith, but it doesn't really represent Jesus until it is moving and speaking.

There are times you may have felt down because you haven't done enough with your faith. This kind of thinking is not from God. You don't earn your salvation through works; your salvation has already been given to you through Jesus. But you can become a beautiful example of Christ when you choose to act out your faith through your good actions and kind deeds.

ACT OF KINDNESS

Leave a nice note on someone's car.

Good Morning

> "The greatest love of all is a love that sacrifices all. And this great love is demonstrated when a person sacrifices his life for his friends."
>
> John 15:13 TPT

Take a moment to think about the kind of love Jesus showed people. The love of Christ was filled with sacrifice; he let go of his own desires to meet others' needs. We are born to be self-preserving, which means that we naturally do things to protect ourselves. So we might give some, but we don't give too much.

It will likely take a lifetime to truly understand what giving your life for someone else really looks like. Thankfully, Jesus gave us the perfect example. He was full of humility, kindness, and self-control. He is the source of love. Look to his light and let his kind of love shine through you to others.

ACT OF KINDNESS

Text three friends, "Good morning."

Call Your Mother

> "How could a loving mother forget her
> nursing child and not deeply love the one she bore?
> Even if a there is a mother who forgets her child,
> I could never, no never, forget you."
>
> ISAIAH 49:15 TPT

Do you sometimes get so busy that you forget about the people around you? Mothers might be forgetful at times, but they don't usually forget their children. On the rare occasion they do, God reminds you that he never forgets. He is the perfect parent who will always look out for your needs.

Some of us have family who are reliable, and others might not. Take some time to pray about your mother, or a mother figure, and your relationship with her. Pray that it gets even better or that you can find another wise woman in your life who can help be that form of comfort to you.

ACT OF KINDNESS

*Call your mom (or a mother figure in your life)
and tell her how much you appreciate her.*

overlooked

Jesse sent for his son and had him brought in.
He looked very healthy. He had a fine
appearance and handsome features.
Then the LORD said, "Get up and anoint him.
This is the one."

1 SAMUEL 16:12 NIRV

When Samuel went to find the new king of Israel, Jesse first showed him all the children he thought would be suitable for the job. But God had other plans. He didn't care about age or skill; he was looking at the heart.

You might be someone who feels like you are overlooked a lot. It could be your age, the way you look, or your education. Those things do not matter at all in God's eyes. He looks at your heart and thinks you are amazing because you were created in his image. You might know others who are ignored for similar reasons. Spend some time praying for them today and encourage them with kind words.

ACT OF KINDNESS

Tell someone's parent how great they are.

ValUE Of TWO

As iron sharpens iron,
so one person sharpens another.

PROVERBS 27:17 NIV

Do you have a friend you can have meaningful conversations with? There are some friendships you put a lot into, but they don't seem to get better. You might hang out together for a while, but at the end of the day, you just don't feel that great.

Then there are those friendships where you challenge each other with new ideas, try to think of the Bible in a different way, or talk about how you might change the world for good. Hold on to these friendships and make time for these people. Let yourself be sharpened by friends who are as loving, thoughtful, and creative as you are.

ACT OF KINDNESS

Make two lunches: one for you and one to give away.

PRESENT HELP

> God is our place of safety. He gives us strength.
> He is always there to help us in times of trouble.
>
> PSALM 46:1 NIRV

We are living in a world full of distrust. In times when we should be able to turn to authorities for help, we are even questioning them. Our police force may not be perfect, but there are so many men and women who have dedicated their lives for the good of others and who have honest and good intentions.

Take some time today to put aside your feelings and pray for those who are trying to help in a very broken world. No one is perfect, and no one does their job perfectly. Pray for encouragement, wisdom, and truth for our justice system.

ACT OF KINDNESS

Bring cookies or treats to your local police station.

Control Yourself

God will never give you the spirit of fear,
but the Holy Spirit who gives you mighty power,
love, and self-control.

2 TIMOTHY 1:17 TPT

There are way too many things in life that make us feel
angry. We might lose our patience with a sibling who keeps
arguing back or with a puppy that has dug too many holes!
There are times when our friends might say something
unkind, and we talk back with more harsh words.

In the moments you are calm, take a minute to think about
what triggers your responses. Is it because you are worried
for that person, you don't like messes, or you are insecure
about your friendship? Think about the real issues and ask
the Holy Spirit to guide you away from fear and toward his
love. Figure out some ways, before you get angry, to avoid
losing control.

ACT OF KINDNESS

Let someone go ahead of you in line.

Nagging

It is better to live in a desert
than to live with a nagging wife
who loves to argue.

PROVERBS 21:19 NIRV

Does this verse make you feel a little of regret over the way you argued with someone lately? There might be good reasons to continue to ask someone to do something: teachers remind students to hand in assignments, parents remind children to clean their rooms, and siblings remind each other whose turn it is to go first.

Nagging is different than just reminding, and sometimes it can be annoying. But our best response is to just get the job done. Or if we're the ones who need something done, we can find a more polite way of asking instead of being irritating. Take a step back and send a prayer to heaven. It will be more effective if the Holy Spirit gives others a tap on the shoulder for you.

ACT OF KINDNESS

Finish a task someone has been asking you to do.

Lending

Whoever is kind to the poor lends to the Lord,
and he will reward them for what they have done.

PROVERBS 19:17 NIV

Have you dropped a few coins in a donation box lately or given your allowance to a child from a third world country? Just when you think you have done your good deed for the year, you get asked to do more. Before you respond negatively, take a moment to consider this verse.

What if it were Jesus asking you to give just a little bit more to help someone get food, shelter, or medicine? Would you say no? You shouldn't feel like you have to give more than you have, but giving a little extra will help you see where your treasure really is. Imagine the reward of Jesus smiling down on you and saying, "Thank you. I love you."

ACT OF KINDNESS

Put some coins in the offering at church.

Tip On Tips

> You must each decide in your heart how much to give.
> And don't give reluctantly or in response to pressure.
> "For God loves a person who gives cheerfully."
>
> 2 CORINTHIANS 9:7 NLT

The end of a dinner out means thinking about a tip. When we are told we must pay a tip, it doesn't feel like we are doing it out of gratitude.

You don't have to give a lot all the time, but it might go a long way to making someone's day if you decide to be generous, maybe even to someone who you don't think deserves it. Think of the times when you have experienced an unexpected gift. The provision of Jesus reminds us that he knows our needs and he will take care of us.

ACT OF KINDNESS

Put a tip in the tip jar.

smokes and mirrors

> Put on all of God's armor so that you will be able to stand firm against all strategies of the devil.
>
> EPHESIANS 6:11 NLT

Have you ever been to a magic show or seen a trick that you know doesn't make sense, but it still seems to have happened? Our hearts and minds can also believe false truths if we do not protect ourselves against doubt. The devil has a plan to make you doubt that God is real, or question his goodness, or maybe even make you lose faith in yourself.

When you look in the mirror, God wants you to see his truth about you. You are excellent, you are unique, and you are loved. Make sure to put on the armor that declares his truth over your life and be ready to stand firm against the lies of the devil.

ACT OF KINDNESS

Put an encouraging sticky note on a bathroom mirror.

Battle

You equipped me with strength for the battle;
you made those who rise against me sink under me.

PSALM 18:39 ESV

When you hear stories or read books about war, it feels like a lifetime away, but there are people alive today who had to serve in the military to protect our freedom. We might not face physical wars, but we have our own battles with those around us, and we even experience battles in our hearts and minds.

War is often about power and money. Our personal struggles are different, but God still equips us with the strength to face the battles so we can conquer evil. Surrender yourself to him today.

ACT OF KINDNESS

*Say thank you to an active military member
or veteran today.*

JUNE

Be kind and compassionate to one another,
forgiving each other,
just as in Christ God forgave you.

EPHESIANS 4:32 NIV

Abiding Love

> If anyone has the world's goods and sees
> his brother in need, yet closes his heart against him,
> how does God's love abide in him?
>
> 1 JOHN 3:17 ESV

Have you ever read a really good book, or watched a great movie, and then kept thinking about it all day almost as if you were one of the characters or like the plot actually happened to you? Why not let the story of Christ consume your heart today?

Find some time to read a chapter or watch a Bible story and then put yourself in that story. Let yourself hear Jesus as if he were speaking directly to you. Imagine yourself watching the others around you as they hear Jesus. Imagine seeing one of your friends being healed. We are in the story of Christ whether it is written down or not. As you place yourself in this story of faith, let the love of Jesus spill out into your actions for others. Be Jesus to those around you.

ACT OF KINDNESS

Read a story to someone younger than you.

There Your Heart Is

"Where your treasure is, there your heart will be also."

MATTHEW 6:21 ESV

Think about the things that make you happy. It could be your family and friends, an instrument you play, the bike you just got, or your favorite sport. We put our time and energy into so many things, and it pays to stop and ask what we really value.

If you feel like you might be putting your time into the wrong things, spend a few moments recommitting your heart to Jesus. Let the Holy Spirit speak to you about what is important to him right now. Let him guide you toward the things, and the people, that really matter. Respond by treasuring your relationships and letting the love that Jesus has put in your heart shine through.

ACT OF KINDNESS

Invite a friend over for lunch.

Moved by Compassion

When Jesus came ashore, he saw a large crowd. He felt deep concern for them. They were like sheep without a shepherd. So he began teaching them many things.

MARK 6:34 NIRV

When Jesus saw the crowds, he didn't just see them as an annoying group; he saw them as people with needs. Like sheep without a shepherd, people are lost, and they need our help. Sometimes the needs are obvious like help with a newborn or food for the hungry. Other needs are deeper like the need to have a friend or to be healed from emotional pain.

Jesus has compassion! And because we know this loving Jesus, we can have compassion for others too. He is able to help with your needs and he will give you the strength to help others in theirs.

ACT OF KINDNESS

Help your parents clean the house.

Not Helpless

The LORD gives sight to those who are blind.
The LORD lifts up those who feel helpless.
The LORD loves those who do what is right.

PSALM 146:8 NIRV

Our God loves to restore life to his creation. When Jesus came to earth, he healed many physical needs, restoring people to health. But greater than physical healing is that Jesus came to restore the brokenness of our spirit. He opened eyes to the truth, ministered to the poor in spirit, and restored believers to righteousness.

How blessed you are, that he has opened your eyes, that he will always lift you up in times of trouble, and that he loves you because you have chosen the path of righteousness. Let the God of encouragement and healing give you strength to encourage others who might be feeling sad today.

ACT OF KINDNESS

Bring a treat to a friend.

Added Learning

Instruct the wise and they will be wiser still;
teach the righteous and they will add to their learning.

PROVERBS 9:9 NIV

The writer of these words knew that a wise person is not just one who has a lot of knowledge. The wise person is one who listens to instruction; they always look for wise ways. A righteous person is one who wants to add to the truth they already know.

Is your heart open to learn? Do you want to add to your knowledge of the truth of God's Word? God is happy that you pursue him. He will instruct and teach you to be wiser when you ask for it.

ACT OF KINDNESS

Share a good book with a friend.

SOW PEACE

Those who make peace plant it like a seed.
They will harvest a crop of right living.

JAMES 3:18 NIRV

Peaceful ways are the beginning of righteousness. There are times when conflict cannot be stopped, but always try to take the role of the peacemaker instead of getting your own way. To be a peacemaker requires humility. One of the many names of Jesus is the Prince of Peace. He is our best example of what it means to make peace. He lives in you and when you pray, he will give you strength to bring peace in times of conflict.

Think of a situation that seems troubling to you right now or think of a person who seems troubled. Allow the Holy Spirit to give you ways to bring peace into either situation.

ACT OF KINDNESS

*Give away your spot in line
by letting someone go first.*

God Created

God saw everything he had made.
And it was very good. There was evening,
and there was morning. It was day six.

GENESIS 1:31 NIRV

There's no doubt when you look at all the incredible creatures of the world, there must have been a mastermind behind it all. It doesn't really matter what you believe about the origins of creation: God created it all. You only have to watch the Discovery Channel to be absolutely stunned by the amazing detail and intelligence of nature.

Take some time to appreciate the mysterious ways of God. They are seen in things you don't understand, but also in simple things that you do. Notice the color of a flower, enjoy feeling the softness of a dog's ears, listen to the song of the early bird. When God created, it indeed was very good.

ACT OF KINDNESS

Bring treats to a dog park.

All-Powerful Cross

I trust in the all-sufficient cross of Christ alone.

1 CORINTHIANS 1:17 TPT

This verse frames the wisdom of the past, present, and future. Jesus' suffering, death, and resurrection is the wisdom of God. It is also God's power to redeem all. Healthy eating, fitness routines, or breaks from media show us how we try to better our lives. Good role models give us little bits of wisdom to help us make better choices. But the wisdom Paul speaks about is eternal.

Wise sayings and good advice can touch the present, but how much better is wisdom that strengthens the eternal soul. That kind of advice starts with God's gift on the cross. As you grow in wisdom, grow your trust in the gift of the cross and encourage others to receive life gifted by a good Creator and Father.

ACT OF KINDNESS

Write an encouraging note and tuck it in someone's book.

Bearing It

By helping each other with your troubles,
you truly obey the law of Christ.

GALATIANS 6:2 NCV

One of the best things about close friends and family is that you can count on them to help you in your troubles. It wouldn't take you long to think of a time when you were upset or feeling sad and were able to talk to someone who really cared for you. And you help others with their trouble when they need to talk. This is a simple law of Christ: to love others as you love yourself.

You will be blessed by helping others, but perhaps you can think of ways you can help even more. Can your school help another school out? Can your church help another charity in your area? Can your family offer support to another family in need? You have room to think big in God's kingdom.

ACT OF KINDNESS

Listen to a friend who needs to talk.

orderly

Everything should be done in a fitting and orderly way.

1 Corinthians 14:40 NIV

The kind of order the Scriptures are talking about here is church meetings and what was going on at that time. Order helps keep things from getting out of control and gives people some guidance and peace about what is going to happen. Sometimes people feel better about their situation when the space around them is clean and tidy.

Our physical environment can have a lot to do with how we are feeling. Take a moment to look at the space you are in right now and think about whether you need to clean or put yourself in a more peaceful environment.

ACT OF KINDNESS

Vacuum a shared space.

Shared Skills

God has given each of you a gift from his great variety of spiritual gifts. Use them well to serve one another.

1 PETER 4:10 NLT

Do you like to draw, or read, or play an instrument? If you think about things you enjoy, you can probably remember when you started to learn how to do them. God has gifted everyone with talents and skills, and it is a pleasure to pass the skill along to others.

Thank Jesus for the gifts you have received and for the teachers who helped you develop them. It is a joy to master something we didn't know how to do before and experience satisfaction when we create something beautiful. The community of learning and passing it on is truly God inspired.

ACT OF KINDNESS

Teach someone something you know.

Discovery

If we keep living in the pure light that surrounds him, we share unbroken fellowship with one another, and the blood of Jesus, his Son, continually cleanses us from all sin.

1 JOHN 1:7 TPT

Have you ever watched the Discovery Channel and marveled at how little you know about the planet? There are so many things to discover about God's creation and it can be mind-blowing when you learn something you never knew. It can be even more overwhelming when you think about the rest of the things you don't know!

We serve the God who created all things, and he understands everything perfectly. Each person God created has their own look, character, and experience. There is so much to know about each other, and for the sake of better relationships it is good to get to know people on a deeper level.

ACT OF KINDNESS

Find out something new about a friend.

Gray Ways

Gray hair is a crown of splendor;
it is attained in the way of righteousness.

PROVERBS 16:31 NIV

With each passing year, we gain experience and understanding. At some point, we will all have gray hairs and wrinkles. These are signs that we have journeyed through life with God at our side. We will go through joys and pains; we will make mistakes and rise above them. We will learn how to find peace and strength to endure and appreciate what we have learned about God, ourselves, and others.

There is always someone older and wiser than you; they have just gleaned that wisdom a little earlier than you have. Take some time to listen and learn from those who are older than you.

ACT OF KINDNESS

Call a grandparent and tell them you love them.

TOO MUCH

> "Everything I've taught you is so that the peace which is in me will be in you and will give you great confidence as you rest in me. For in this unbelieving world you will experience trouble and sorrows, but you must be courageous, for I have conquered the world!"
>
> JOHN 16:33 TPT

Sometimes we say yes to too many things. You might have agreed to help someone work on their school project, volunteered to help out at the next church event, and still have your own homework and chores to do.

When we find ourselves in these situations, we don't have peace because our minds and bodies haven't been able to do something relaxing. Ask the Holy Spirit to help you figure out what needs to be done and learn from this time to say no to things when you know you already have a lot going on.

ACT OF KINDNESS

Smile at someone.

In Every Way

In every way we show we are servants of God:
in accepting many hard things, in troubles,
in difficulties, and in great problems.

2 CORINTHIANS 6:4 NCV

It's easier to be nice when things are going well for us. Sometimes the sun is shining on all that we do, and we go out of our way to make others feel loved and accepted. But what are we like when we are having a hard time? Troubles cause stress, and stress can make us less gracious, less patient, and sometimes just simply unkind.

Look at your heart today and see if the hard things you are facing are stopping you from showing grace to others. Ask Jesus to heal your heart and help you to be more loving with those around you.

ACT OF KINDNESS

Give someone in your family a foot massage.

Get Together

When we get together, I want to encourage you in your faith, but I also want to be encouraged by yours.

ROMANS 1:12 NLT

There is something wonderful about meeting in person. It sets the tone for a good time. You probably have a lot of conversations during your day, but it is good to meet in person with those who help you in your faith.

Take some time to hang out with a Christian friend and share what God has been teaching you. Ask them questions. Don't be afraid to talk about your doubts and concerns too. Invite Jesus into your time and watch how you grow as you experience the joy of getting together.

ACT OF KINDNESS

Do something fun with a friend.

TOIL

> That each of them may eat and drink,
> and find satisfaction in all their toil—
> this is the gift of God.
>
> ECCLESIASTES 3:13 NIV

What is it that occupies most of your day? You might be focused on schoolwork, practicing your music or sport, and spending time with friends. Or maybe you have chores around the house and need to look after your siblings. There are so many things God has given people to do: jobs that are both paid and unpaid.

Even though we will not always enjoy our jobs, they are giving back to the place we live in. Take some time to think about how your chores contribute to others. Find some satisfaction that your work is not in vain. And don't forget to enjoy the tasks you complete. This is a gift from God.

ACT OF KINDNESS

*Hand out water bottles to people
who are working outside.*

Bound Together

> Above all, clothe yourselves with love,
> which binds us all together in perfect harmony.
>
> COLOSSIANS 3:14 NLT

Do you sometimes wonder about the way the church is set up, how it works, and why we meet every week? As we face all kinds of uncertainty, it does us good to think about things we often take for granted. Even if the government stops us from meeting together, we are still a part of the church.

You might have felt obligated to go to church, but when it is taken away, you realize how truly precious being with other believers is. Aside from your thoughts on worship, sermons, and volunteering at church, can you see that it really is love that keeps us together? Meet in person when you can because it is a way to share in the love of God.

ACT OF KINDNESS

Help someone with their kids during a church service.

Three Things

Until then, there are three things that remain: faith, hope, and love—yet love surpasses them all. So above all else, let love be the beautiful prize for which you run.

1 CORINTHIANS 13:13 TPT

What do you hope for most in life? Is it beauty, a good job, to get married, to have children? Do you want to do something unique like write a book or come up with a new invention? These are all important. And we all have gifts to use that can help us achieve them. They are God-given gifts, so don't ignore them.

When it comes to the kingdom of heaven, there is really nothing that is more important than your faith, hope, and love. This Scripture tells us that love is above everything else. It was the love of God that created us, the love of Jesus that saved us, and the love of the Holy Spirit that keeps reminding us that we are loved. Walk in this love today.

ACT OF KINDNESS

Help your parents make lunch.

Never-ending Feast

> For the despondent, every day brings trouble;
> for the happy heart, life is a continual feast.
>
> PROVERBS 15:15 NLT

A lot of our life comes down to how we look at it. A dropped bowl of cereal could make us angry, but it could also make us laugh. A cancelled sports practice could be seen as a frustration or a welcome opportunity to take a break.

Ask Jesus to help you approach your day with a positive mind and heart. Work on not making big things out of little things and appreciate the small blessings in your life. Turn your lemons into a lemonade!

ACT OF KINDNESS

Make someone laugh.

Inheriting the Wind

Those who trouble their households will inherit wind,
and the fool will be servant to the wise.

PROVERBS 11:29 NRSV

Do the people in your house talk about their emotions,
or are you in a family that keeps things to themselves?
Neither way is wrong, but there are times when we can be
a stirrer of trouble in our homes. We might be in a grumpy
mood that sets the tone for a tense dinner. We might argue
just because we like to. We might tease someone about
their new haircut.

Families are full of trouble, but they can also be our best
source of joy. Take some time to enjoy the people you live
with today. Thank God for bringing them into your life and
figure out what you can do to be a peacemaker.

ACT OF KINDNESS

Do a chore for someone in your house.

Improved With Age

Do not cast me off in the time of old age;
do not forsake me when my strength is spent.

PSALM 71:9 NRSV

Nobody looks forward to getting old, yet there is
something so wonderful about those who have spent so
much time on this earth. Our older generation has seen
many things change over their lifetime; they are able to
remember what the world used to be like, and they can
see how the future is already developing. In a way, they are
closer to being like God than anyone.

The next time you have an opportunity to be with an older
person, listen carefully to their stories and appreciate the
life they have lived. Pray that God would continue to use
them to strengthen and give hope to the next generation.

ACT OF KINDNESS

*Pick flowers for an older person in your family
or neighborhood.*

In Balance

To set high standards for someone else,
and then not live up to them yourself,
is something that God truly hates.
But it pleases him when we apply
the right standards of measurement.

PROVERBS 11:1 TPT

Businesses will do almost anything they can to make money. This means that they may offer discounts and then keep you hooked with more special offers. We should be wise about spending our money and think about what kind of business we put our money into.

These days, a lot of businesses give back to the community in some way. They might be trying to be more environmentally responsible, or they give their leftovers to the poor. Supporting a business that gives back to your community is one way of being a light in this world. Let God's love shine in all different kinds of ways.

ACT OF KINDNESS

Tell someone they are doing a good job.

Skillful Workers

> Do you see any truly competent workers?
> They will serve kings rather than
> working for ordinary people.
>
> PROVERBS 22:29 NLT

When you think of someone who you really enjoy seeing or hearing, who comes to mind? There are many people who have skills, but what makes someone really shine at school or in a social setting? It is probably more about the way this person makes others feel. They might be great listeners, good encouragers, or they work well in a team environment. They might help people get things done.

Too often in life we see the proud people get rewarded instead of those who serve. Ask God to give you character so you are recognized for the right things.

ACT OF KINDNESS

Send a thank you text to someone.

Stones and Embraces

A time to cast away stones,
And a time to gather stones;
A time to embrace,
And a time to refrain from embracing.

PROVERBS 22:29 NRSV

The wisdom of God is not always black and white. For example, saving your money might be the right thing to do one time, but it might be just as right to give your money in another. In the same way, a hug might be appropriate when a friend needs comforting, but it maybe wouldn't be appropriate during a pandemic. This is why Scriptures refer to seasons and times.

Consider the season you are in right now and ask the Holy Spirit to let you know what is right to do. Is it time to be present and listen to a friend who is hurting, or is it time to celebrate with them?

ACT OF KINDNESS

Celebrate someone today.

Great and Small

> "Aren't five sparrows sold for two pennies?
> But God does not forget even one of them."
>
> Luke 12:6 NIRV

Some people may think that animals are the least important of God's creation. But God created everything to work in harmony. Without trees we would not have oxygen, without crops we would not have food. Animals have their purpose too. We have pets to protect, to be companions, or to calm anxiety. Animals are a part of God's kingdom and should be treated as valuable to God.

This Scripture says not one of God's creatures is forgotten by him. Take some time to care for his created world today.

ACT OF KINDNESS

Donate tennis balls to your local vet.

Already Done

> "You have already been cleansed by the word that I have spoken to you."
>
> JOHN 15:3 NRSV

Sometimes we keep falling into the same sin over and over again. We might have asked for forgiveness for our temper, but then we find ourselves yelling again the next day. We might have apologized for sleeping in one day, but still rush every morning and make others late.

There are a lot of reasons you might continue to feel unworthy or unclean. But God doesn't see your mistakes the way you see them. He sees you as forgiven. You don't need to work hard for your freedom, you have already been set free.

ACT OF KINDNESS

Help clean up someone's room.

COME EAT

"Listen! I am standing at the door, knocking;
if you hear my voice and open the door,
I will come in to you and eat with you,
and you with me."

REVELATION 3:20 NRSV

You know those times you hear the welcome words of a parent telling you it's time to eat? There is something about being hungry, waiting for food, and then finally getting to have a meal that is so fulfilling.

Sometimes we don't know how to ask for what we really want, but Jesus knows what that is. He could be standing at your door right now, knocking and hoping you hear his voice. What is it you want? What are you hungry for? Let Jesus in and allow him to share this moment with you.

ACT OF KINDNESS

Help make dinner tonight.

surprise

> The kingdom of God is not a matter of talk.
> It is a matter of power.
>
> 1 CORINTHIANS 4:20 NIRV

Do you like surprises, or do you prefer to be in control of your plans? The kingdom of God was not anything like people expected it to be. When Jesus arrived, he came as a baby, and he didn't act like a king who ruled with force. Jesus showed his power in ways that helped others. He healed people, he gave them confidence, and he left the gift of eternal life.

The kind of love Christ has shared with us is powerful. Love is not just about words; its power goes well beyond that. Surprise someone today with a powerful act of love.

ACT OF KINDNESS

Surprise a friend with a gift.

Words that Build

When you talk, do not say harmful things,
but say what people need—words that will
help others become stronger. Then what you say
will do good to those who listen to you.

EPHESIANS 4:29 NCV

There are words that build people up and words that bring people down. We can be unkind with a harsh text, or a few mean remarks behind someone's back. We might not like someone, so we choose not to tell them something they need to know.

If you are older than others, your words have a greater impact. Ask Jesus to give you a kind heart that flows with thoughtful words.

ACT OF KINDNESS

Say something nice to the first person you see today.

JULY

Use your freedom to serve
one another in love.

GALATIANS 5:13 NLT

GOOD NEWS

> He said to them, "Go into all the world and proclaim the good news to the whole creation."
>
> MARK 16:15 NRSV

Sharing good news does not mean you need to have a stage or a platform or even a speech prepared. Jesus shared the good news through conversation. He got to know people and talked with them about their needs. He listened and he cared.

The good news of Christ is that death is not our end. In fact, it is the very opposite. Jesus promises eternal life. He wants us to live to the fullest today. Let this fill you with joy and peace so your words and actions can bless those around you.

ACT OF KINDNESS

Tell a friend about Jesus.

Fill the Tank

You prepare a table before me in
the presence of my enemies.
You anoint my head with oil;
my cup overflows.

PSALM 23:5 NIV

Enemies are not just people. Attacks can come in different forms, and sometimes we are even like enemies to ourselves. Our world is so full of things to see and do that we can become worried we are missing out. We can also get depressed when we start to compare our lives to others.

Maybe you don't feel great about school, or you haven't found good friendships. These kinds of things can leave you feeling a little empty. Jesus can fill your tank! Talk with Jesus today and ask him to show you what really matters. Count up all the small blessings and you will soon see that your cup is actually overflowing.

ACT OF KINDNESS

Pour a drink for someone in your house.

Fishing Coins

> "We don't want to upset these tax collectors. So go to the lake and fish. After you catch the first fish, open its mouth and you will find a coin. Take that coin and give it to the tax collectors for you and me."
>
> MATTHEW 17:27 NCV

This story about Jesus almost feels funny. Jesus had been asked if he needed to pay tax and he responded in a way that showed who he really is. But Jesus wasn't trying to brag about his ability to find money in a fish's mouth. He chose not to be offended and supported the earthly system of taxes.

Imagine finding a coin in the mouth of a fish! This is sometimes the way Jesus works through us. You might be going through a difficult decision. Follow the example of Jesus: don't upset people if you don't need to; expect him to provide what you need for the situation. He will show up.

ACT OF KINDNESS

Drop a few quarters on the sidewalk for people to find.

Heroes

> Bear one another's burdens,
> and so fulfill the law of Christ.
>
> GALATIANS 6:2 ESV

When things start to go really wrong in our world, there are men and women of courage who have been trained to help. These people are not better humans than anyone else, but they have made a decision to put themselves on the front line for the people around them. They protect our rights and our freedom.

This is the kind of sacrifice and burden that Jesus carried for us, so we didn't have to carry the weight of our own sin. His life paid the price and now we are free. Thank God for the people in our lives and our communities who continue to do that for us.

ACT OF KINDNESS

Bring cookies or treats to your local fire station.

Working Hands

> Make it your goal to live a quiet life,
> minding your own business and working with
> your hands, just as we instructed you before.
>
> 1 Thessalonians 4:11 NLT

What are the kinds of jobs you really love doing? You might enjoy reading, solving puzzles, and studying, or you may prefer to do things like building, drawing, or crafting. We were all made with things to enjoy and sometimes even the jobs are fun because we like to make something with our hands.

Spend time doing the things you love so you keep busy and happy with those things instead of being lazy. Boredom often leads to trouble. If you can't think of things to do, think of what you can do for others. No matter how small it is, all of our work is meaningful.

ACT OF KINDNESS

Wipe down the counter or table.

Love Perfected

Such love has no fear, because perfect love expels all fear. If we are afraid, it is for fear of punishment, and this shows that we have not fully experienced his perfect love.

1 John 4:18 NLT

We are usually rewarded for good behavior and punished for bad behavior. This makes us want to do the right thing. The love of Jesus goes beyond right and wrong. His love does not depend on the choices we have made. It is unconditional.

You might be holding onto guilt for something you have done in the past, and maybe you fear what the end result might be. You might expect to be punished sometime later. This is not living in perfect love. Be confident that Jesus loves you no matter what you do: past, present, or future. Because of this perfect love, you will be inspired to choose the right thing!

ACT OF KINDNESS

Give someone an encouraging card.

All Circumstances

> Be thankful in all circumstances,
> for this is God's will for you who
> belong to Christ Jesus.
>
> 1 THESSALONIANS 5:18 NLT

It's easy to be thankful when things are going really well. There are seasons when you enjoy life, like maybe you had a great summer vacation with the family. These are things to be grateful for. What about the times you have heard bad news? While those times can be hard, they are also what draw us closer to God.

As you ask him to be there for you, remember to first be grateful for the goodness he has already shown you. As you think of things to be thankful for, you will feel your spirit lift. Be encouraged and then be encouraging to others around you.

ACT OF KINDNESS

Thank someone with a text.

NO PLACE

"Foxes have dens and birds have nests,
but the Son of Man has no place to lay his head."

LUKE 9:58 NIV

Jesus knew what it was like to be without a home. He knew what it felt like to be on the outside without something of his own. Do you know anyone who has struggled financially? There are all kinds of reasons that people are homeless, but it's not something we should judge. Instead, we should feel compassion for them and smile; be nice even just for a moment.

You can't save the world, but you can bring light into it, one person at a time.

ACT OF KINDNESS

Give a snack to a friend.

Have-nots

The generous will themselves be blessed,
for they share their food with the poor.

PROVERBS 22:9 NIV

Even though we might not mean to complain, we often point out that our friends have more than we do. They have their own phone, or a bike, or go on better vacations. These comparisons make us feel like we are less because we have less.

Instead of worrying about not having everything, make it your goal to be generous. Be someone who is quick to donate a can of food at the store or drop a few coins in a donation bucket. This will give you more blessing than you could ever get by simply wishing that you were someone who had more.

ACT OF KINDNESS

Donate canned food to your nearest foodbank.

Called to Serve

You, my brothers and sisters, were called to be free. But do not use your freedom to indulge the flesh; rather, serve one another humbly in love.

GALATIANS 5:13 NIV

Jesus freed us from all sin. We should live without being weighed down by sin and guilt. And our joy and freedom should be shared.

The love you feel from Christ should be spread to those around you. You don't have to do this with fancy words or by proving that you are a better person than others. You can simply share the freedom you have by cheerfully serving those around you and accepting people as they are.

ACT OF KINDNESS

Tell someone that Jesus loves them.

Shining Deeds

> "In the same way, let your good deeds
> shine out for all to see, so that everyone
> will praise your heavenly Father."
>
> MATTHEW 5:16 NLT

Do you remember building a fort in your room and using a flashlight to see under the blankets? Maybe you are more of a camper and have sat inside a tent with a dim light playing games. You know that a light can only go so far as the material you put around it.

When you are hiding under those blankets, the light will be useful for you, but not anyone else in the room. When you do something good or helpful for someone else, you are letting God's light go beyond yourself and into the world. Your kindness helps others see the goodness of our Creator.

ACT OF KINDNESS

Help a sibling or friend build a fort.

Waste Not

My dear brothers and sisters, stand strong.
Do not let anything move you. Always give yourselves
fully to the work of the Lord, because you know that
your work in the Lord is never wasted.

1 CORINTHIANS 15:58 NCV

The world needs people doing small, good things to make it a better place. You might hear the news and worry about all the problems. There is not one person or company that could solve all the issues. We need so many people doing what they are passionate about to actually make a difference.

You might not be leading a big charity or be able to contribute much to your local food shelter, but there are so many other ways you can make a difference. Ask the Holy Spirit to guide you with those actions today.

ACT OF KINDNESS

Offer to clean out a friend's room.

Know God

> Anyone who does not love does not know God, because God is love.

1 John 4:8 nirv

What have you learned about God lately that you didn't already know? You might know the simple truths: that he died for you, forgives you, and loves you deeply. This would be enough to know about him, but he shows himself in so many other ways.

Consider how you see God in other people, in nature, or over time. You can get to know him through the Bible or in daily conversations with him. Make it your goal to know more about God. The more you experience his love, the more you will be able to love others.

ACT OF KINDNESS

Pick flowers for someone.

Everlasting Life

> "This is how much God loved the world—
> he gave his one and only, unique Son as a gift.
> So now everyone who believes in him will
> never perish but experience everlasting life."

JOHN 3:16 TPT

It's important to recognize how much changed when God gave up his Son, Jesus, to make things right again for us. Jesus showed us what God was like through his words and actions when he was on earth. Jesus came as a human to set us free from the consequence of sin. Jesus defeated death for us!

We will experience eternal life because of what Jesus gave us. Let the thought of everlasting life encourage you with whatever you might be experiencing today.

ACT OF KINDNESS

Invite a friend over.

POWER OF LOVE

Hatred stirs up trouble,
but love forgives all wrongs.

PROVERBS 10:12 NCV

We will experience hurt from other people in our lives. Sometimes this hurt is on purpose, and other times it is because we just don't agree on everything. We fight or argue with people, and we want to be right. This is why it is important to talk with Jesus when you are feeling hurt by someone.

Jesus will continue to remind you of the love and grace you have experienced from him. He knows that love will forgive all wrongs even though forgiveness is hard. It brings freedom. Let God help you on your journey of healing as you learn the power of love.

ACT OF KINDNESS

Give your friend a list of things you love about them.

welcome me

> "I was hungry and you gave me food,
> I was thirsty and you gave me something to drink,
> I was a stranger and you welcomed me."
>
> MATTHEW 25:35 NRSV

Do you remember what it felt like to be the new person in school, church, or a neighborhood? It can be very lonely when you don't have a friend to share your time with.

We don't always know where to turn for help. When people reach out to us, it is such a relief. Jesus knew what it was like to be in need, and he showed gratitude to those who fed him and welcomed him in. Is there someone new at your school, church, or street who needs to feel welcomed by you?

ACT OF KINDNESS

Tell someone you love them.

presence

> You will show me the way of life,
> granting me the joy of your presence
> and the pleasures of living with you forever.
>
> PSALM 16:11 NLT

It doesn't always feel like life is full of God's presence. Sometimes it feels like the opposite. Many of the psalms share the feelings of the times when God seems far away, and it's important to acknowledge these as real emotions. The truth is that God is always near.

Sometimes our darkest times can turn into our closest times with our Creator. If you are feeling far away from him right now, ask him to give you the joy of his presence and allow your heart to be filled with the thought of living with him forever one day.

ACT OF KINDNESS

Leave a card on your dad's desk.

Have Courage

"Here is what I am commanding you to do.
Be strong and brave. Do not be afraid.
Do not lose hope. I am the LORD your God.
I will be with you everywhere you go."

JOSHUA 1:9 NIRV

We are always fighting something. Our fight isn't with swords and shields, but we have to defend ourselves from negative people and bad thoughts almost every day. Sometimes we let the situation overwhelm us and that leads to a lot of unnecessary stress.

When you are in this frame of mind, you need to take courage in the form of a command from the Lord. He is with you wherever you go. He is on your side, and he will make sure you can stand in the face of your battles. Stand strong and inspire others to do the same.

ACT OF KINDNESS

Write an encouraging note to someone.

Trust Him

> The Lord is my strength and my shield;
> in him my heart trusts;
> so I am helped, and my heart exults,
> and with my song I give thanks to him.
>
> PSALM 28:7 NRSV

When was the last time you really needed help? You might have needed someone to help you understand your homework or needed instructions to the right classroom. Perhaps you needed help with your attitude or sleep habits.

Whatever your needs are, God knows them, and he is there to help. The next time you feel like you don't know where to start, get on your knees and pray. Let God into every area of your life so you can figure it out together. When you get the help you need, you will be able to praise him and trust him even more.

ACT OF KINDNESS

Help out in the kitchen.

Delight in Relationship

Make God the utmost delight and pleasure of your life,
and he will provide for you what you desire the most.

PSALM 37:4 TPT

What would you say you want most right now? Your
thoughts might jump to a new phone, a better toy, or
maybe even something as simple as a bowl of ice cream!
Those things will make you feel better for a moment, but
when you take time to think about what really makes
you happy, you will soon realize that you care more
about friends you can trust, healthy family members, or a
peaceful home.

Relationships are what matter most, and you will find
this when you make God the delight of your heart. Your
relationship with him will grow and so will your ability to
relate well with others.

ACT OF KINDNESS

Send a letter to someone.

Wish List

> "I tell you, whatever you ask in prayer,
> believe that you have received it,
> and it will be yours."

MARK 11:24 ESV

Prayer doesn't change God's mind; it changes our hearts. Some people think the verse above means you can ask God for whatever you want, and he will give it to you. This isn't how it works. You might have prayed for God to stop that test at school from happening, but when you showed up, the teacher was still there handing out the test papers. Or you may have prayed for instant healing of a sickness, and it still took weeks to recover.

The power of prayer is that the more you keep praying, the more you keep believing and the more you submit to God's will. It might not be the answers you started praying for, but you will receive what you need.

ACT OF KINDNESS

Pray for a friend or family member to be blessed.

Deliver Me

I prayed to the LORD, and he answered me.
He freed me from all my fears.

PSALM 34:4 NLT

What are you worrying about right now? Is it a test, a
project, or a sick friend? This world is full of concerns, and
you are not alone in facing anxiety. Times of pressure can
bring your deepest fears to the surface.

You might be afraid of failing, afraid of not getting good
grades, or of losing someone you care deeply about. These
are very real fears, but they can be brought to the Lord
who understands your fears and wants to carry them for
you. Imagine yourself as that mail person who delivers a
package and lightens their load. Bring your package of fear
to the Lord and let him carry it for you.

ACT OF KINDNESS

Thank your mail carrier.

Real Time

Let the words you speak always be full of grace.
Learn how to make your words what people
want to hear. Then you will know
how to answer everyone.

COLOSSIANS 4:6 NIRV

Have you ever caught yourself in a conversation that is
almost all about television shows or celebrities? We can
get so caught up in the celebrity world that we stop paying
attention to what is happening in the real world around us.
We might care more about catching the next episode than
asking a friend or someone from our family how they are
doing.

The next time you are in a conversation, be a little more
aware of what you are talking about. Try to center your
words around the person you are with and what they are
experiencing. Focus on things that help encourage and
show grace to whomever you might be discussing.

ACT OF KINDNESS

*Put your phone away when you're spending time
with a friend.*

Multiplied

> He ordered the crowds to sit down on the grass.
> Taking the five loaves and the two fish,
> he looked up to heaven, and blessed and
> broke the loaves, and gave them to the disciples,
> and the disciples gave them to the crowds.
>
> MATTHEW 14:19 NRSV

The story of the bread and fish is a great reminder of what Jesus can do with our simple offer to help. A few loaves of bread and fish was all a small boy had to offer a crowd of thousands, but that didn't stop him bringing it to Jesus. There are many times we doubt that what we have will be enough.

The feeling of not being enough is made worse by comparing yourself to others. We only know about having more or being better because we are looking at what others have. Take some time to consider what you have to offer Jesus. Remember that he sees the willingness of your heart as the miracle starter. Bring what you have and watch him multiply it for good.

ACT OF KINDNESS

Make lunch for someone.

unconditional

Christ proved God's passionate love for us by dying in our place while we were still lost and ungodly!

ROMANS 5:8 TPT

Have you ever worried about giving money to someone who might waste it? Maybe you have held back from saying something nice to somebody who already thinks very highly of themselves. It's hard to be kind all the time.

It's true that things are not always right or wrong, and we have to be smart about how we give. But remember that the love we experience from Jesus each day has nothing to do with us earning it. Grace isn't really amazing unless it is undeserved. Be kind today whether you want to or not!

ACT OF KINDNESS

Stick a few quarters to a candy machine.

Cling to Good

Love must be sincere.
Hate what is evil;
cling to what is good.

ROMANS 12:9 NIV

It is normal to face difficult times by focusing on the problem and how it makes us feel. While it is good to be able to understand our emotions, it can also overwhelm us if we think about those emotions for too long. One of the best ways to get out of a dark place is to do something good for someone else.

Don't just fake a smile; bring joy to someone else in a more meaningful way. Don't stop doing good; every small piece of goodness will make a positive difference to your heart and mind.

ACT OF KINDNESS

Help bake someone a cake.

GOD'S KIDS

See what kind of love the Father has given to us,
that we should be called children of God; and so we are.
The reason why the world does not know us is
that it did not know him.

1 JOHN 3:1 ESV

What does it mean to you to be called a child of God? You might be growing up in a house with a single parent or moving between your parents' homes. Your family situation is different to others. It is a different experience than what your friends have. In God's house, however, we are all the same. We are all loved unconditionally and deeply cared for by God.

The world might not understand what it's like to be living under God's roof, and you can expect to be misunderstood or thought of as different. As you live out your faith, the world will begin to see the peace you have from knowing you are a part of God's family. When you get the chance, let others know they can be a part of this great family too.

ACT OF KINDNESS

Tell someone about how awesome God's family is.

Love Cover

> Hatred stirs up quarrels,
> but love makes up for all offenses.
>
> PROVERBS 10:12 NLT

There will be people in our lives who we just don't like very much. You can probably think of a person you don't get along with. It might be someone at school, church, or maybe even a family member. Sometimes it's hard to find something you both like, and sometimes you just annoy each other. Maybe someone is loud, rude, or only talks about themselves.

Jesus didn't ask us to like people, but he did say we should love them. When we don't like someone, we find things to argue about with them, or we talk behind their backs. Love is what makes you realize you need to choose to forgive when you have been hurt. Choose love, not because it will make you like the person but because it keeps you from being filled with anger.

ACT OF KINDNESS

Choose to forgive someone who has hurt you.

Loyalty

Never let loyalty and kindness leave you!
Tie them around your neck as a reminder.
Write them deep within your heart.

PROVERBS 3:3 NLT

Who do you go to when things get tough or when you just want an honest opinion about something? Usually we have a close friend or family member we can share with. These are the people you can talk to without fear of judgment. They love you and they will stick by you no matter what.

Hold onto these people and these moments like precious jewels. In the same way you rely on them, they will need to rely on you as well. Leave time and space to show your care and kindness to one another.

ACT OF KINDNESS

Send a card to a close friend or family member.

Never Give Up

Love never gives up, never loses faith, is always hopeful, and endures through every circumstance.

1 Corinthians 13:7 NLT

You might not feel like you are the best example of Christ's love even though you know this is one of the greatest commandments. Don't worry; you are not alone. It is hard to know where to begin sharing God's love. You might hope that someone will ask you about it one day. You might decide to say something but then lose courage halfway through the day.

Keep praying and working on your relationship with Jesus so you feel blessed by your faith. Recognize that it is Jesus who helps you to never give up, to be hopeful, and to make it through every hard time. Ask Jesus to help you come up with a way to talk about your faith.

ACT OF KINDNESS

Write out an encouraging Scripture and leave it on someone's desk or bed.

All You Do

Be loving in everything you do.

1 CORINTHIANS 16:14 NIRV

What are mornings like for you? Do you wake up feeling more tired than when you went to sleep? Are you the first one up at your house? You might feel anxious about the day ahead, or simply just want to get breakfast so you can start your day.

Think about some friends in your life who are probably going through similar feelings and routines. While many of us feel like we have to get up, make it a habit to be grateful that you get to wake up. While there is still life in your body, take some time to focus on the positive and keep doing all that you do in love.

ACT OF KINDNESS

Text three friends, "Good morning."

AUGUST

"They are blessed who show mercy to others,
for God will show mercy to them."

MATTHEW 5:7 NCV

Filled With Laughter

> He will once again fill your mouth with laughter
> and your lips with shouts of joy.
>
> JOB 8:21 NLT

A good laugh makes your heart happy. When was the last time you laughed so hard your face hurt? Sometimes all it takes to end an argument is a joke. You have to pick your moment, but sometimes instead of continuing to argue, you could just make a silly face or a dumb joke. You might be surprised how quickly a situation turns around.

Remember that Jesus experienced all of our human emotions. We were created with mouths full of laughter and lips ready to shout for joy.

ACT OF KINDNESS

Send a funny meme to a friend.

Help Please

> How does God's love abide in anyone
> who has the world's goods and sees
> a brother or sister in need and yet refuses help?
>
> 1 John 3:17 nrsv

You only need to take a look around your home to know how blessed you are. Being able to have breakfast, pour yourself a cup of juice, and get into some clean clothes are a few of many things you can do that others cannot. You don't need to feel bad about the things you have, but you should be grateful for them.

Every time you think of complaining, remember that there are people who have almost nothing. Think of how much God loves them and wants their needs to be cared for as well. Put that love into action.

ACT OF KINDNESS

Donate food to your local homeless shelter.

Love Your Neighbor

> "'You must love your neighbor in the same way
> you love yourself.' You will never find
> a greater commandment than these."
>
> MARK 12:31 TPT

When the Bible talks about your neighbor, it means everyone around you, but what have you done for your actual neighbor in a while? Sometimes life is so busy that we barely see the people on our street. We might wave when we are leaving the house, but that could be all we do.

It's a lot easier to do things for people you know really well. It's a little harder to do something for people you are not close to. This is where we can rely on our helper, the Holy Spirit, to fill us with good thoughts toward those we don't know. He can help us to love our neighbors as ourselves.

ACT OF KINDNESS

Bring in your neighbor's garbage can.

Heartfelt Advice

Perfume and incense bring joy to the heart,
and the pleasantness of a friend springs
from their heartfelt advice.

PROVERBS 27:9 NIV

Have you noticed how good some stores smell? The scent of brownies, vanilla, cologne, or fresh flowers draws you in and probably makes you want to buy something. A friend should feel like that pleasant scent. The words you share with each other can be comforting and understanding. A friend who truly loves you will accept you for who you are and what you say, but even more than that, they will help guide you into a good place. Friends don't let each other continue in harmful behaviors or hang out in bad environments.

If you don't feel like you have a friend like this, pray for one. Think of your friends who need your kind words during this time in their life.

ACT OF KINDNESS

Ask a friend how they are doing.

Feed the Flock

> Let us consider how to stir up one another
> to love and good works.
>
> HEBREWS 10:24 ESV

There is power in numbers. Sometimes we can be pulled the wrong way by what most people are saying or doing. When we hear that our friends are not going to a certain event because they can't be bothered, or our teammates aren't interested in starting a task the team was asked to do, we want to join the group, but what if they are wrong?

There is strength when everyone says yes, so think about how you are able to stir up others to do good works. What have you been asked to do lately that might mean doing something you'd rather not even though you know it's a good thing to do?

ACT OF KINDNESS

Say yes to volunteering for something at church.

NO CONDEMNATION

> "Judge not, and you will not be judged;
> condemn not, and you will not be condemned;
> forgive, and you will be forgiven."

LUKE 6:37 ESV

It's easy to look at other people's mistakes and faults. We seem to like talking about what is wrong with people rather than what is right. Maybe your parents talk about your strengths and gifts. They might be more gracious toward your mistakes because they love you so much. Do they try to understand you and give you a chance to explain yourself? They might try, but they aren't perfect.

Your heavenly Father is perfect, and he loves you unconditionally. God sees you as his child; he sees the best in you and his grace is never ending. Choose to see others through his eyes today.

ACT OF KINDNESS

Choose to have a judgment-free day.

Wonderfully Made

> I praise you because I am fearfully
> and wonderfully made;
> your works are wonderful,
> I know that full well.
>
> PSALM 139:14 NIV

It's easy to marvel at God's creative work when you see a newborn baby. They are perfect. As we get older, we start to see all the things we don't like about ourselves. You might not like your curly hair or short legs. You might be terrible at sports or not very musical. You might also wonder why God didn't make you as smart as your sibling. These thoughts creep in so often that it is good to remind ourselves of who made us.

God made you fearfully and wonderfully. His works are great! Find something you can marvel at today and make sure to praise God for the beauty that you find.

ACT OF KINDNESS

Tell someone they are wonderfully made.

Donkey Problems

If you see that your neighbor's donkey or ox has collapsed on the road, do not look the other way. Go and help your neighbor get it back on its feet!

DEUTERONOMY 22:4 NLT

When was the last time you were asked to clean up your room, or clean up a mess in the classroom even when it wasn't your mess? Did you say, "But I didn't do that!" This is true, but it is also the way a community works. We don't have to make a mess or problem to be a part of the solution. Just because someone threw some trash on the side of the road, doesn't mean you shouldn't pick it up.

God wants us to work together, and you are playing your part every time you help make this world a little bit better. If your neighbor has a problem, help them; don't look the other way. If someone falls down, pick them up again.

ACT OF KINDNESS

Sweep your neighbor's driveway.

Blessed to Give

I have been a constant example of how
you can help those in need by working hard.
You should remember the words of the Lord Jesus:
"It is more blessed to give than to receive."

ACTS 20:35 NLT

Did you wake up this morning already feeling tired? It can often feel like our days are just full of work. We get ourselves dressed, go to school, do homework, and then practice an instrument or sport before eating dinner and going to bed. Free time doesn't really feel like a thing anymore.

Jesus is your strength. He is with you ready to give you new energy. Remember his words, as we are told in this Scripture, that it is more blessed to give than to receive. Every time you help others, consider yourself blessed because you are able to give.

ACT OF KINDNESS

Drop off snack at someone's house.

In the Ordinary

The LORD has done it on this day.
Let us be joyful today and be glad.

PSALM 118:24 NIRV

Today might feel like an ordinary day. You might have started the day feeling great, but now you aren't in a very good mood. In these moments it's good to take a deep breath and remember this is the day the Lord has made. Think of the things you have to be grateful for.

Sometimes it takes the low moments to seek God for things you can be glad about. At some point in your day, or week, you are going to feel a little bit better than you are right now. Hold onto the promise that your Creator wants you to enjoy your days, through all of the emotions you might experience. Give someone else that hope by reminding them of things to be glad about.

ACT OF KINDNESS

Tell someone you are praying for them today.

Admirable

> No one is abandoned by the LORD forever.
> Though he brings grief, he also shows compassion
> because of the greatness of his unfailing love.
>
> LAMENTATIONS 3:31-32 NLT

You might look at certain actors or people on stage at church and wish you looked, talked, or played an instrument like them. But even those people have others they compare themselves to. We often want to be noticed and try to be better than others instead of finding our worth in Jesus.

The Lord does not abandon anyone, and his unfailing love means that you will never be forgotten or thought of as less than perfect. Be confident in who you were created to be and show your confidence by admiring others for their unique talents.

ACT OF KINDNESS

Send a thank you email to someone you admire.

It's Not Instant

> The Holy Spirit produces this kind of fruit
> in our lives: love, joy, peace, patience,
> kindness, goodness, faithfulness.
>
> GALATIANS 5:22 NLT

When you assess the list of this Scripture, does it make you feel like you aren't living up to a standard? You might quickly think of a time when you didn't show joy or patience. This does not mean that you are not living out your faith. The fruit on a tree takes time to develop; it comes after hard seasons and times of growth.

Remember that the Holy Spirit is always working in you. Keep asking for guidance and strength. The fruit is something that will develop as you go. When the time comes for that fruit to appear, make sure to put it on display and offer it as a gift to others.

ACT OF KINDNESS

Smile at the person in the car next to you.

Walk Surrendered

> Continue to walk surrendered to the extravagant love of Christ, for he surrendered his life as a sacrifice for us. His great love for us was pleasing to God, like an aroma of adoration—a sweet healing fragrance.
>
> EPHESIANS 5:2 TPT

We always seem to be in a rush to get somewhere. We leave ourselves very little time on either side of our activities. If we have a spare moment, we fill it with another task or event. Sometimes we have to stop the things we want to do for the sake of someone else. Perhaps you are just about to sit down and do your homework and a friend arrives to talk about a hard day.

Little interruptions can be a disruption, but you can see them as an opportunity to share the love of Jesus. The sacrifice to let someone's need come before your own is a sweet fragrance to the Lord.

ACT OF KINDNESS

Let someone in front of you in line.

Grace Upon Grace

> From his fullness we have all received,
> grace upon grace.
>
> JOHN 1:16 NRSV

If you live near the ocean or remember the last time you visited it, you will know the pleasure of seeing wave after wave roll onto the shore. Sometimes it is a gentle wave, and other times they are loud and powerful waves that crash onto the shore with grand effect.

Just like the ocean, the grace of Jesus is forever rolling in, wave after wave. Sometimes we just need the gentle reminder that things are okay, and other times we have gotten so stuck in our sin that we need a more powerful wave of grace to wash us thoroughly. The grace of Jesus is life changing and for everyone. Extend that grace to the people in your lives today.

ACT OF KINDNESS

Write down three things you love about someone in your family, and then deliver the message.

AMONG US

The Word became human and made his home
among us. He was full of unfailing love and faithfulness.
And we have seen his glory, the glory of
the Father's one and only Son.

JOHN 1:14 NLT

What is your picture of Jesus? Is he some mysterious force
that sits in the heavens, the Jewish baby born in a manger,
or the man who did miracles and sat with sinners? Jesus is
all of these and he wants to be known by you. He did not
come to earth just to rule and reign, he also came to be
with us. He experienced all kinds of human emotions and
he helped people not only with supernatural power but
with his kind words and actions.

We have seen the Father through Jesus and the more we
know Jesus, the more we can be his hands and feet to the
people around us.

ACT OF KINDNESS

Offer to help with someone's kids.

Like Eagles

Those who hope in the Lord will renew their strength.
They will soar on wings like eagles;
they will run and not grow weary,
they will walk and not be faint.

Isaiah 40:31 niv

When you have a lot going on, there are times you want to just lay on the couch or your bed for some much-needed rest. Our emotions are connected to our energy levels. Thinking happy thoughts can actually make you feel better.

God gives us hope, and he offers a life that is better than anything this world can give. When you understand his love and the great future he has promised for you, you can't help but rise up in hope. Let this hope give you energy, so you are ready to pass on happiness to those around you.

ACT OF KINDNESS

Say something nice to someone.

Humility

Love is patient and kind. Love is not jealous,
it does not brag, and it is not proud.

1 CORINTHIANS 13:4 NCV

This is a very popular Bible verse, and we can all agree that love is shown when we are patient, kind, and humble. But what about those times when patience and kindness are not in our words and actions? What about those days we feel grumpy, and our answers are impatient or unkind?

In those times, remember this: God is love. He is patient, he is kind, and he is merciful. Take in some of the grace your Creator has for you. It is God within you who helps you to conquer your feelings of jealousy and pride. It is God who helps you to love.

ACT OF KINDNESS

Compliment someone in front of other people.

COUNT IT UP

Love is not rude, is not selfish, and does not get upset with others. Love does not count up wrongs that have been done.

1 CORINTHIANS 13:5 NCV

Sometimes it is hard to see love in this world. People are rude and selfish, and we get upset a lot. It's hard not to get mad when we have been treated unkindly. When we are hurt by someone, it is helpful to ask what they are going through. Maybe the other person is afraid, hurt, tired, or simply hungry.

God loves us even when we behave poorly, and while we shouldn't let others walk all over us, it's always better to ask God for understanding. Forgiveness helps us get rid of the wrongs that we might be tempted to add up.

ACT OF KINDNESS

Tell someone's parents how great they are.

Belonging

> This is how we know that we belong to the truth and how we set our hearts at rest in his presence.
>
> 1 John 3:19 NIV

How do we know what is true? The only truth we can depend on is the truth found in God's Word. He tells us that we belong to him. In a world where we are trying to figure out our place, fit in with certain groups, or share common interests, we can often feel lonely.

God's truth is that you are a part of his family, and nothing is going to change that. As you think about how you belong to God, let your heart rest in his love.

ACT OF KINDNESS

Do a chore for someone in your house.

Obligation Free

You must each decide in your heart how much to give.
And don't give reluctantly or in response to pressure.
For God loves a person who gives cheerfully.

2 Corinthians 9:7 NLT

Money is really hard to let go of. Many people don't have a lot of it, and it isn't very often that we feel like there is extra to hand out. The Bible tells us to listen to our hearts when it comes to giving. If your heart is generous toward something, then give to it.

When you give because you want to and not because you feel like you have to, you will be blessed with joy. This is the delight of a cheerful giver! Give when your heart tells you to, and when it does, give bravely, give generously, and give with joy.

ACT OF KINDNESS

Invite someone over for dinner.

Right Expectations

His divine power has given us everything we need for a godly life through our knowledge of him who called us by his own glory and goodness.

2 PETER 1:3 NIV

We are taught about doing the right thing and being honest in the community and around our friends. When we fail to do this, we can be hard on ourselves. Our desire to do the right thing should come from wanting to please God. If it comes from anywhere else, it is not right.

The Bible says that our godly life comes through knowing Jesus, through his power, and through his goodness. Trying to live a good life on our own is never going to work. We have to trust Jesus and let him give us what we need to choose the right things.

ACT OF KINDNESS

Say thank you to a parent.

Salvation to All

The grace of God has appeared that
offers salvation to all people.

TITUS 2:11 NIV

In a stadium full of people, you will often see groups of
people wearing a team color. It could be easy to think that
Christians should be one color and everyone else another.
But God wants all people to be saved. He wants us all on
the same team.

It is sad that many people do not know that freedom is
just a prayer away. If we know that Jesus' grace is given
to all, we should do our best to be an example to others
through gracious acts and words, so they want to come
join our team.

ACT OF KINDNESS

Bring a neighbor a batch of cookies or treats.

Be Courteous

Remind them to never tear down anyone with their words or quarrel, but instead be considerate, humble, and courteous to everyone.

TITUS 3:2 TPT

We should be inspired by great leaders, but we also need to careful about who we are following. If your leaders are tearing people down with words and fights, perhaps they are not the Christlike example you want to follow.

Always look to Jesus for examples of how to live, talk, and treat others. Be considerate, humble, and courteous to everyone. Sometimes this might simply mean that you don't say anything unless you can share it humbly. We need to listen to the voice of the humble.

ACT OF KINDNESS

Include someone in a conversation who usually doesn't have much to say.

Learn about Me

"Simply join your life with mine. Learn my ways and you'll discover that I'm gentle, humble, easy to please. You will find refreshment and rest in me."

MATTHEW 11:29 TPT

When was the last time you sat down and had a conversation with Jesus? Our prayers are often the kind that ask for help when things get hard. We might have a test at school or an important recital, so we invite the Holy Spirit to be with us. This is all great communication with God, but have you considered listening to what he might be saying to you?

God wants to have deep connection with you. He wants to hear what is on your heart, and he wants you to discover that he is gentle and easy to please. The next time you pray, find some time to listen to God's response.

ACT OF KINDNESS

Write a kind prayer on a mirror or whiteboard for someone in your house.

LOVE ON DISPLAY

He has made everything beautiful in its time.
Also, he has put eternity into man's heart,
yet so that he cannot find out what God has done
from the beginning to the end.

ECCLESIASTES 3:11 ESV

A small seed is not very beautiful. Neither is the dirt the seed is put in. The roots begin to form, and they don't look like what the plant will be. The rose has the same humble beginning as any other plant, but it becomes beautiful in its time. This is also what God does in our hearts.

We might not see a lot of beauty in our lives, but God is aware of the seed that he has planted. He knows he created you to live for eternity and as you discover more of his kingdom, you will become more a part of it. Your beauty will be clearer in time. Hold onto the promise that you are part of his plan and invite others into that plan through your actions of love.

ACT OF KINDNESS

Pick flowers for your mom.

Ways to Unite

> He makes the whole body fit together perfectly.
> As each part does its own special work,
> it helps the other parts grow, so that the whole body
> is healthy and growing and full of love.
>
> EPHESIANS 4:16 NLT

The life of the church has gone through so many changes, but it never goes away. This is because the Church is what Jesus is using to bring man to God. There are a lot of reasons you might not like church, but we need to remember that Jesus loves the Church as his bride.

It is sad when Christians and churches begin to fight; it is not what God wants. Find time to pray for your church and encourage other believers.

ACT OF KINDNESS

Donate toys to your local church.

Fight Bravely

Be courageous! Let us fight bravely for our people and the cities of our God. May the LORD's will be done.

2 SAMUEL 10:12 NLT

Watching the news can make us feel hopeless. We see stories of people whose lives have been ruined by many things. The lives of those who are weaker need protection, and that can come from those who are strong enough to help.

This is the time to be courageous: to stand up for those who are weak and hurting. Fight bravely for these people. Pray, offer practical help, and watch the love of God change lives, cities, and nations.

ACT OF KINDNESS

Help your dad clean the car.

Daily Cross

> "If any of you wants to be my follower,
> you must turn from your selfish ways,
> take up your cross daily, and follow me."
>
> Luke 9:23 NLT

If we think about how Jesus suffered and died for us, it can fill us with great sadness. It should also bring incredible gratefulness, knowing that his whole life was committed to bringing us into relationship with him.

What do you picture when you are asked to take up your cross and follow Jesus? Perhaps you feel like your life is hard every day. Following Jesus has a cost, but it also leads us to freedom from sin and death and gives us power over evil. As you follow Jesus today, remember that while it may be hard, your commitment leads you to the path of victory.

ACT OF KINDNESS

Give away something for free.

Handiwork

> The heavens tell about the glory of God.
> The skies show that his hands created them.
>
> PSALM 19:1 NIRV

It only takes one look at the endless sky to know that life is bigger than what we experience on earth. A limited understanding of the solar system can leave us amazed, as can a brilliant display of stars on a clear night. The work of God's hands is awesome.

Does this sound like the God you know? He is so glorious and powerful, and yet he is also so near and detailed. What can you see around you that shows the work of his hands? Allow yourself to dwell on how creative God is and be encouraged that this same God created you. Take time to notice God's glory in the people around you.

ACT OF KINDNESS

Tell a friend or family member how beautiful they are.

Proactively Positive

I make one more appeal, my dear brothers and sisters. Watch out for people who cause divisions and upset people's faith by teaching things contrary to what you have been taught. Stay away from them.

ROMANS 16:17 NLT

On social media, you might hear more negative things than good. Unfortunately, being able to hide behind a keyboard and not own up to what we say, means that there are thousands of unkind words typed without a care for how it will make others feel.

Even if we are not a part of writing those words, we read them a lot, and they can influence how we think. Listen to the caution of this verse and watch out for people who cause divisions. This is not the healing work of Jesus. Be part of his kindness and be positive toward others.

ACT OF KINDNESS

Post a compliment on your friend's social media.

Brought Low

> Pride brings a person low,
> but the lowly in spirit gain honor.
>
> PROVERBS 29:23 NIV

Welcome to Christ's upside-down kingdom! In this life, we think about proud people as being successful in the world's eyes. The problem with having pride in worldly things is that they are temporary.

This is not what God wants for us. He wants us to be proud of how he has created us on the inside. You are beautiful regardless of what position the world might put you in. Remember it is those who don't think so highly of themselves that will gain honor. Help give someone an extra boost today with a kind word.

ACT OF KINDNESS

Tell someone how much you love them.

SEPTEMBER

"Love your enemies, do good to them, and lend to them without hoping to get anything back. Then you will have a great reward, and you will be children of the Most High God, because he is kind even to people who are ungrateful and full of sin."

LUKE 6:35 NCV

Inner Strength

I pray that, according to the riches of his glory,
he may grant that you may be strengthened
in your inner being with power through his Spirit.

EPHESIANS 3:16 NRSV

What things are stressful for you at home? It could be that
you are not getting along with someone, and this is making
it hard to be kind. A very popular saying tells us that home
is where the heart is. Where is your heart right now?

Your family relationships matter more than your
surroundings. Ask the Holy Spirit to give you strength from
the inside out and let this strength guide you toward health
in your relationships.

ACT OF KINDNESS

Tell a family member what you like about them.

A Parent's Sacrifice

Train up a child in the way he should go;
even when he is old he will not depart from it.

PROVERBS 22:6 ESV

Parents have it pretty rough! It doesn't matter what stage of life a child is in, whether a newborn, a toddler, or a teenager, the work is hard, and the responsibility is great. Parents, of course, take on this burden because they love their children incredibly and want what is best for them.

It isn't easy to be thankful for what your parents are trying to do for you, or to understand what is involved in the decisions they make for your wellbeing. One day you might understand, but for now, try to encourage your parents rather than arguing with them. No parent or child is perfect, but we are all created in the image of God, and we deserve to be encouraged to do the best job we can.

ACT OF KINDNESS

Thank a parent for taking care of you.

Perfect Gifts

Every generous act of giving, with every perfect gift,
is from above, coming down from the Father of lights,
with whom there is no variation or shadow
due to change.

JAMES 1:17 NRSV

Have you ever gone shopping for a friend or family member and didn't know what to get them? You might be looking for the perfect gift, but nothing seems to stand out as exactly the right thing. This is kind of what it's like to look for your joy outside of the gift of Christ. Nothing will fill you the way the grace and forgiveness of Jesus will.

You can trust Jesus; there is nothing to worry about. He has completely accepted you for who you are, and you are free because of his work on the cross. When we live with the promise of Jesus in our hearts, our giving is also perfect. This doesn't mean you will find the perfect gift, but it means that your heart of giving will be the perfect light shining through to those who receive it.

ACT OF KINDNESS

*Buy or make a gift for someone just
because you think they are awesome.*

Thriving

The eyes of all look to you in hope;
you give them their food as they need it.

PSALM 145:15 NLT

Indoor plants can be hard to take care of. You might have a family member who knows exactly where to put a plant or how to make it thrive, but many of us don't quite know how to keep it alive!

Just like plants, our spiritual growth is determined by whether we are receiving all the right things. We need to be nourished by the Bible and receive plenty of light from the love of Jesus. Look to him in hope and he will give you everything you need. Notice the things that make you thrive and make sure to keep them as a routine in your life.

ACT OF KINDNESS

Help someone take care of their plants.

Virtual Holes

I gain understanding from your precepts;
therefore I hate every wrong path.

PSALM 119:104 NIV

When was the last time you got lost on social media? You might have clicked on one friend's video and then got caught by an ad or picture on someone's else's post and pretty soon you found yourself having spent over an hour of wasted time!

We need to be careful when we are browsing online. Take this Scripture and apply it to the social media paths you are going down. Make it your goal to look for the things that have meaning and add value to your life and the lives of others. Stop yourself from going down paths that are not headed in the right direction. God's Word will give you the best understanding of what is good and right.

ACT OF KINDNESS

Write a positive comment on social media.

JOYFUL JOBS

They seldom reflect on the days of their life,
because God keeps them occupied
with gladness of heart.

ECCLESIASTES 5:20 NIV

Is it possible for us to view work as a gift? Whatever God
has given you to do, whether in a classroom, church, or at
home, he has given because you have a gift that is to be
used for others and for his glory.

Be encouraged that you can find joy in knowing you
are doing part of what God created you to do. Have
satisfaction in the jobs you have right now. Allow God to
bring you enjoyment through your gifts and share them
with those around you today.

ACT OF KINDNESS

Help a friend out with a task they need to finish.

Riches Of Wisdom

My fruit is better than fine gold;
what I yield surpasses choice silver.
I walk in the way of righteousness,
along the paths of justice,
bestowing a rich inheritance on those who love me
and making their treasuries full.

PROVERBS 8:19-21 NIV

The way rich and famous people live seems pretty nice. We are drawn toward being the best or having the most. What is valuable to the world is not what impresses God, instead he asks us to pursue wisdom.

The book of Proverbs continually compares wisdom and understanding to precious metals and stones. This is because the value of wisdom goes well beyond things we can buy with money. Being wise will lead to rich relationships, good decisions, and positive attitudes toward life. Let yourself soak in the gold of God's wisdom.

ACT OF KINDNESS

*Write a Proverb on a piece of paper and
leave it on the kitchen table.*

Persuading Leaders

Use patience and kindness
when you want to persuade leaders
and watch them change their minds
right in front of you.
For your gentle wisdom will
quell the strongest resistance.

PROVERBS 25:15 TPT

When we want someone to change their heart, we should try to approach them with kindness and patience. If we try to shame people into changing, or harm them if they don't, it will not change a thing. Being respectful will go a lot further.

This is especially true with leaders. Whether or not we agree with how our leaders are acting or handling matters, the Lord has put them in their role, and he alone can see their hearts. We should offer them our respect and try to change them with kindness.

ACT OF KINDNESS

Tell your parents something you appreciate about them today.

YOUR OWN GOOD

> We do not enjoy being disciplined. It is painful at the time, but later, after we have learned from it, we have peace, because we start living in the right way.
>
> HEBREWS 12:11 NCV

Discipline is more than correction for doing something wrong. Discipline is a way of training the mind, body, or spirit. Perhaps you have put yourself through some kind of boot camp, or signed up for weekly training, or committed to reading the Bible daily.

You probably know discipline as a reminder of right and wrong, rewards and consequences. It's hard work to get things right, but once you do, it becomes much more natural. Be encouraged that God uses discipline for your benefit. Discipline brings peace!

ACT OF KINDNESS

Encourage a younger child.

Next Steps

We can make our plans,
but the LORD determines our steps.

PROVERBS 16:9 NLT

Someone may have great ideas of their dream home and may even be able to draw some good pictures of it, but eventually it is the builder who determines how to build it and with what materials. Our God is the great builder, and he knows each step we need to take in order to build our lives into something beautiful.

As this Scripture says, we can make our plans, but we need to put those plans in the hand of God and ask him how to begin. What are the steps God might be directing you to take right now? Are there some of your own plans you need to give up so he can work through you?

ACT OF KINDNESS

Do a favor for a family member who is busy.

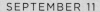

Land Of the Living

I remain confident of this:
I will see the goodness of the LORD
in the land of the living.

PSALM 27:13 NIV

The Bible says that God has set eternity in our hearts.
Sometimes we long for heaven instead of enjoying the
life he has given us to live on earth. Be confident like the
writer of this psalm and tell your soul that you will see the
goodness of God in the land of the living.

Determine to spend time with people who will energize
you and challenge you to live life more fully. Spend time
in God's Word so your heart is grounded in the hope and
love of Christ. Listen to some music and appreciate all the
different instruments you can hear. Enjoy some good food.
Be grateful for all the blessings that you have on earth.

ACT OF KINDNESS

Invite someone to listen to music with you.

Good Stored Up

> "A good man brings good things out of
> the good stored up in him, and an evil man
> brings evil things out of the evil stored up in him."
>
> MATTHEW 12:35 NIV

We can choose to be good or bad. It all depends on what we feed our bodies, hearts, and minds. As we get older, we make choices that either feed good things or evil things. We might put people down at school so we look better, or enjoy gossiping about others to make ourselves feel better. The more someone feeds these bad habits and stores them in their mind, the easier they come out.

Be encouraged! We can decide to feed our minds and hearts with good things. We can stop negative talk about others. We can volunteer for a charity even when we don't have a lot of time. We can think kind thoughts about our friends or family members so the first thing we say to them is something nice. Keep storing up the good, so good things are always ready to come out of you.

ACT OF KINDNESS

Compliment someone on the way they look.

COMPANY KEPT

> Don't let anyone fool you. "Bad companions make a good person bad."
>
> 1 CORINTHIANS 15:33 NIRV

Friends have the power to influence us. Look at your friends and see who you will be in a couple of years. Good friends are the best way to keep out of trouble and keep working hard at school.

Are the people you spend time with helping you to be a better person, better worker, or a better friend? You might like certain people, but if they are always bringing in unhealthy words or habits, it might be time to pick new friends. Ask the Holy Spirit to guide you toward people who encourage you in truth and kindness.

ACT OF KINDNESS

Send a thank you card to a friend who encourages you toward good habits.

Stop and Ask

> Do not worry about anything, but pray and ask God for everything you need, always giving thanks.
>
> PHILIPPIANS 4:6 NCV

What things cause you to worry the most? Is it your home, your friends, or your parents? We usually have a long list of things we care about and often these worries can lead to anxiety and fear. When you become overwhelmed by worries, it can shadow the truth that God is in control.

There are times when we need to see that we cannot control most of the things we worry about. God is the author of all life, and he knows all situations far better than anyone on earth ever could. The next time worry starts to eat away at you, pray immediately and ask for what you need. Believe that God will provide you with these needs by giving thanks.

ACT OF KINDNESS

Ask a friend how you can pray for them.

Divine Help

In the same way, the Spirit helps us in our weakness.
We do not know what we ought to pray for,
but the Spirit himself intercedes for us
through wordless groans.

ROMANS 8:26 NIV

Have you ever had those moments when you have completely forgotten why you went into a room? You might have to retrace your steps to figure out exactly what you were going to do. This can be what it feels like when we are stuck in a rut in our lives. We aren't sure where to start, and we are not even sure what to ask for. This is when you can rely on Jesus. He knows you and already knows what you need.

In times when you feel lost, remember that the Holy Spirit is right there to help you. You don't even need words, just trust God to step in.

ACT OF KINDNESS

Hold a door open for someone.

Heartfelt Contribution

"Be careful not to practice your righteousness
in front of others to be seen by them.
If you do, you will have no reward from
your Father in heaven."

MATTHEW 6:1 NIV

It doesn't matter how big a gift you can give, what matters
is the heart. Think of the story told in the Bible of the lady
who only had a few coins to put in the offering. While
others laughed at her small amount, Jesus praised her
because she had given all that she had.

You don't need to do more than other people in doing
good just to be seen as the most generous. If your heart
feels compassion toward a person or a cause, simply give
out of that goodness even if it is only something small. God
will use any amount to further his kingdom.

ACT OF KINDNESS

Help a busy teacher with a task.

Rejoice Again

Always be full of joy in the Lord.
I say it again—rejoice!

PHILIPPIANS 4:4 NLT

It is impossible to always express joy on the outside. Imagine if you had to smile all day long, or spend hours laughing; you would be very tired. The joy of knowing Jesus is a different kind of joy. It is a deep feeling of peace because you have the right view of life.

There are always going to be times when we feel like nothing is going our way. But the joy of the Lord means that you are confident he will carry you through the hard times. Your gift of salvation and eternal life cannot be taken away. Let this be the joy that you walk around with every single day.

ACT OF KINDNESS

Smile at three people you don't know.

ASK TO RECEIVE

"Until now you have not asked for anything
in my name. Ask, and you will receive
what you ask for. Then your joy
will be complete."

JOHN 16:24 NIRV

Is there something you feel you are missing out on right now? If you could think of one thing that would help you feel better today or this week, what would it be? You might be thinking of some delicious food to cheer you up or a break from all your homework. Perhaps you are lonely and in need of a friend. These are the things that Jesus wants you to ask him for!

Too often, prayer is the last place we go to ask for what we really want. You might not get what you ask for right away but praying will fill your heart with peace and joy and the grace to wait for the things you desire. Ask today in Jesus' name.

ACT OF KINDNESS

Leave a thank you note for your garbage collector.

Home in Christ

Let all who take refuge in you rejoice;
let them ever sing for joy,
and spread your protection over them,
that those who love your name may exult in you.

PSALM 5:11 ESV

It is hard to watch news of people who have to flee their homes to stay in refugee camps. Imagine what it would feel like to leave all of your things behind and move into a camp full of strangers with nothing to really call your own. We can be spiritual refugees as well if we don't allow our souls to find a home in Christ.

We try to fill our lives with things that make us feel better, but these things will not cause us to rejoice or feel safe. Jesus is your guardian, and he is there to protect you. Take some time today to pray for the refugees of this world, that they would find a home. And take some time to allow your heart to find its home in Jesus.

ACT OF KINDNESS

Drop off school supplies at your local school.

Renewed Cheer

When doubts filled my mind,
your comfort gave me renewed hope and cheer.

PSALM 94:19 NLT

There are a lot of things we are not sure of. You might be new to your school or neighborhood trying to figure out all the unknowns. You might be entering a new friendship and don't know how to figure out if it is the right one to pursue.

Our doubts can become hurdles that we think are too hard to overcome. These are the moments when we need to let Jesus fill our minds and hearts. You can keep focusing on fear, or you can choose to let God give you hope and happiness. Let him fill your thoughts with things that are good, loving, kind, and right. Let your heart turn away from doubt. Hit the day with the hopeful message of Christ.

ACT OF KINDNESS

Text some encouraging Scriptures to a friend.

Trusting Confessions

Confess your sins to each other and pray for each other so God can heal you. When a believing person prays, great things happen.

JAMES 5:16 NCV

We all have secrets that we don't want to share. Some of us try so hard to be perfect that we don't want to admit our mistakes. These things need to be brought into the open, not to everyone, but at least to someone you trust who loves you unconditionally.

It is not good for you to hold onto your sins because you cannot experience healing until you have confessed and accepted the freedom from guilt and condemnation. Make sure you can be that kind of friend to someone as well so we can all help ease each other's burdens.

ACT OF KINDNESS

Ask someone how you can pray for them today.

A Parent's Example

> Honor your father and your mother,
> so that your days may be long in the land
> that the Lord your God is giving you.
>
> Exodus 20:12 NRSV

Spend some time thinking about your relationship with your parents and what that has taught you about love, respect, and sacrifice. Sometimes it can be painful because we aren't shown the love and care we deserve. If this is your story, bring hurt to Jesus and ask for the truth of God's love to be shown to you.

If your parents are a great example of putting your wellbeing above their own and loving you all the time, they are a true example of the love of God. Take some time to thank Jesus for them if this is your experience.

ACT OF KINDNESS

Tell your dad (or grandpa) what you love about him.

Back to Health

When they are sick, God will restore them,
lying upon their bed of suffering.
He will raise them up again
and restore them back to health.

PSALM 41:3 TPT

Good health is a very important part of our lives. We might forget to be grateful for it when we are well and instead be consumed and worried about other things. But when we are sick, it causes pain in more than just a physical way. Sickness can lead to sadness, fear, and stress.

Sickness can also be a clear path to the healing power of Christ. Jesus is so near to those who are unwell. He lies with them in their bed, bringing healing to their hearts and minds and hopefully also their bodies. If you are sick, or know others who are, pray this Scripture of hope and promise over them.

ACT OF KINDNESS

Thank a nurse for their service to the community.

All Is Well

Dear friend, I hope all is well with you and that you are as healthy in body as you are strong in spirit.

3 JOHN 1:2 NLT

What do your emails or texts start off with when you send them to friends and relatives? We want the best for the people we love and it's good to say that. People need to know that we care about them especially when they are lonely.

Real conversations are being had less and less and a simple picture is how we catch up on what is happening in someone's life. Make an effort today to reach out to people you know and let them know you care about their health and strength.

ACT OF KINDNESS

Text a friend three things you admire about them.

Childlike

> "Anyone who becomes as humble as this little child is the greatest in the Kingdom of Heaven."
>
> MATTHEW 18:4 NLT

A child trusts quickly, loves boldly, and accepts willingly. This is why Jesus wants us to keep the faith we have as children. It means we have an open heart to trust the promises of God.

Faith means believing that things will work out for the best. Accepting the love of Jesus means we don't have to try to prove our worth to others. We are loved. Allow Jesus to take your doubts and fears away so you can live in the secure future of a life with Christ.

ACT OF KINDNESS

Tape coins around a school playground for kids to find.

Peace Over Greed

Is not the whole land before you?
Separate yourself from me.
If you take the left hand,
then I will go to the right,
or if you take the right hand,
then I will go to the left.

GENESIS 13:9 ESV

Abram and his nephew Lot had been on a long journey together to reach the land that God had promised them. When they got there, Abram had a choice to make; there was good land and there was very good land. Abram chose peace over greed and gave the very good land to his nephew. As a result, God blessed Abram with a lot more.

You may have some choices to make today that will require you to give up something that seems very good for the sake of someone else. Let God bless you as you practice generosity.

ACT OF KINDNESS

*Let someone in your house choose
what movie to watch.*

counted as Right

> He brought him outside and said, "Look toward heaven, and number the stars, if you are able to number them." Then he said to him, "So shall your offspring be." And he believed the LORD, and he counted it to him as righteousness.
>
> GENESIS 15:5-6 ESV

What are you praying for that you feel like God has not given you yet? The story of God's promise to Abram and Sarah reminds us that it isn't about what we say or do that saves us; it is what we believe.

Abram and Sarah might have wondered if God would give them as many descendants as the stars in the sky as they struggled with having even one child in their old age. But what God says is truth, and his Word did not lie. Abram chose to believe and his heart of belief, God said, made him righteous.

ACT OF KINDNESS

Go for a car ride with a family member just to provide company.

Salty

> "You are the salt of the earth. But what good is salt if it has lost its flavor? Can you make it salty again? It will be thrown out and trampled underfoot as worthless."
>
> MATTHEW 5:13 NLT

You are blessed simply because you believe in Jesus and have eternal life. When Jesus was speaking to the disciples, he wanted them to know that this very good thing they had been given needed to be shared.

There is no point to a life in Jesus if we lose the one thing that makes us different from the world. God wants you to live in a way that shows how wonderful salvation is. Your kind words, gentleness, and encouragement can be like salt in an otherwise tasteless world.

ACT OF KINDNESS

Tell your mom (or grandma) what you love about her.

Be Different

"How are you any different from others
if you limit your kindness only to your friends?
Don't even the ungodly do that?"

MATTHEW 5:47 TPT

The world tells us that we should only be kind to people who are kind to us. They say it is ok for us to be rude or mean to those who are unkind. But Jesus has told us something very different.

Jesus wants us to show his love to everyone we meet whether they are kind or not. If we are only kind to those who are kind to us, we are just like the world. When we are kind to people who are mean to us, it shows those people, and others who are watching, what God's love is really like. It is good to have kind friends, and you should show them kindness too, but be kind to people who aren't your friend and watch what God can do.

ACT OF KINDNESS

Pray for someone who has hurt you.

No Offense

"Blessed is anyone who takes no offense at me."

MATTHEW 11:6 NRSV

It can be easy to have a day full of wondering where God is. We can feel attacked when we hear others laugh about Christianity or find a way to blame God for all the wrong in the world.

To the world, the message of Jesus and his death on the cross is offensive. To those of us who believe, we find our true fulfilment in his message because it gives us hope, peace, and joy. Jesus can handle your doubt but ask him to restore your faith, so you know you are living in the truth.

ACT OF KINDNESS

Choose not to be offended today.

OCTOBER

Whenever we have the opportunity, we should do good to everyone—especially to those in the family of faith.

GALATIANS 6:10 NLT

FOUND

"What do you think? Suppose a man owns 100 sheep and one of them wanders away. Won't he leave the 99 sheep on the hills? Won't he go and look for the one that wandered off?"

MATTHEW 18:12 NIRV

Your heavenly Father's love has no limits. There is nothing you can do to change how he feels about you. It's easy to forget we are already perfectly loved, but God loves us more than we can imagine, and he would do anything for us.

Remember this during the day and thank him for caring so much about you. As you show gratitude to him, think of others in your life who are like the lost sheep in this Bible verse and pray that they would find their way to God.

ACT OF KINDNESS

Thank a police officer for their service to the community.

HaVing TOO MUCH

> "When the young man heard this,
> he went away sad. He was very rich."
>
> MATTHEW 19:22 NIRV

Being rich is not all great like we think it should be. The more we have, the more we have to lose. Jesus wanted the rich man to have a compassionate heart—one that was willing to give up what he had for God. This would have meant giving up the life he was used to.

Before asking God to bless you with riches, ask him to bless you with a heart of giving. Thank him for giving you more than enough. Ask him to help you to be content with what you have and to think more of others.

ACT OF KINDNESS

Help someone in your church or neighborhood.

overtime

"You will continue to harvest your grain until you gather your grapes. You will continue to gather your grapes until you plant your crops. You will have all you want to eat. And you will live in safety in your land."

LEVITICUS 26:5 NIRV

It is amazing how busy the world gets during the day. Sometimes we feel like doing homework is not very spiritual, yet God wants us to be productive so we can have a life full of blessing. Whatever type of work you have done today, know that God is pleased with you. Your dedication to doing your part in this world is helping you to be a blessing to your family and to others.

God wants you to feel secure in knowing that he will provide for you. Reflect on the work that you have done today and be encouraged that this is part of God's plan to provide for you.

ACT OF KINDNESS

Offer to do an hour of work for your parents.

Deeply Moved

> When Jesus saw her weeping, and the Jews who had come along with her also weeping, he was deeply moved in spirit and troubled.
> "Where have you laid him?" he asked.
> "Come and see, Lord," they replied.
>
> JOHN 11:33-34 NIV

The story of the death and resurrection of Lazarus was miraculous, but it began with pain. When Jesus learned of his friend's death, he was very sad. Jesus deeply cared for others. Are you able to imagine Jesus weeping with Mary and Martha?

Are you willing to share in the emotions of those around you? The Lord has placed many different people in your life, and each of them go through hard things. Learn to share in the joys and pains of others so they can experience the depth of care from a true friend.

ACT OF KINDNESS

Check in with someone who has lost a loved one recently.

Like Jesus Does

"If I then, your Lord and Teacher,
have washed your feet,
you also ought to wash
one another's feet."

JOHN 13:14 ESV

Jesus showed how great his love was by doing the job
that was only for a lowly servant. He was adored by his
disciples as a great teacher, yet he gladly showed the
disciples his love through an act of humility.

Jesus wants us to show this same humility for one another.
It doesn't matter who we are, we need Jesus' heart of
compassion to serve one another in love.

ACT OF KINDNESS

*Make a foot spa for someone in your house
and massage their feet.*

Forever Love

From far away the LORD appeared
to his people and said,
"I love you people with a love that
will last forever.
That is why I have continued
showing you kindness."

JEREMIAH 31:3 NCV

There are some friends that last forever, and there are others who will be in your life for a short time. You might have become friends with a new student or a neighbor. But seasons change and people move on. Family is never just for a season. Family is forever. They are the ones in the birthday and wedding pictures that you still recognize and connect with. These are the people you should focus your love on.

Just like God has shown us a forever love and never-ending kindness, we should also extend unconditional love, forgiveness, and kindness to our family members.

ACT OF KINDNESS

Write a thank-you note to a family member.

What Joy

Yes, the Lord has done amazing things for us!
What joy!

PSALM 126:3 NLT

It's good to sit down every once in a while and look back over old pictures. Many pictures are taken in good times: during family celebrations, vacations, or big moments.

As you remember these times, thank the Lord for the amazing things he has done for you and your family. Try and remember the good times even if right now those relationships are harder than you would like them to be. Ask God to restore the life of your family so you can celebrate again with each other and exclaim, "What joy!"

ACT OF KINDNESS

Send a fun card to someone in your family.

change your mind

Set your minds on things that are above,
not on things that are on earth.

COLOSSIANS 3:2 ESV

We spend a lot of time alone with our thoughts. The things we fill our heads with often come out in what we say and do. You might feel as though your thoughts just happen, but you can change your mind.

The next time your thinking is negative, either about yourself or someone else, stop that train and get off it. Set your mind on a different course—on the grace of God—and watch it make a difference in how you treat others.

ACT OF KINDNESS

Send a positive message to someone today.

A Wise Fool

Don't fool yourselves. Suppose some of you think you are wise by the standards of the world. Then you should become "fools" so that you can become wise.

1 CORINTHIANS 3:18 NIRV

Are you the kind of person who always has an opinion? Maybe you always have something to say about what is happening at home, school, church, or in someone else's life. You might think you have wisdom or ideas to share that will be useful. It's okay to share your opinion, but it might be better sometimes to just listen.

We can fill ourselves up reading and watching things that support our opinions. This doesn't give us a balanced view of things. Don't let yourself be fooled into thinking you know it all. Submit yourself to listening to the Holy Spirit who will always point you to the truth.

ACT OF KINDNESS

Listen to a friend who needs to talk.

What You Eat

"What goes into someone's mouth does not defile them, but what comes out of their mouth, that is what defiles them."

MATTHEW 15:11 NIV

We judge people based on how they look and act. In Bible times, people were very concerned with the laws that told them what they could and could not eat. They would judge people based on whether they stuck to the rules or not. In our day, we might have certain standards for people like what type of clothes they should wear, how they should talk, or what school they should go to.

The Bible clearly tells us that we cannot judge people with our own standards or ideas. It is what is in people's hearts that really matter, and you can't ever truly know that without knowing them more fully. Leave the judging up to Jesus and choose to love instead.

ACT OF KINDNESS

Choose to have a judgment-free day.

Nourishment

> "Blessed are those who hunger and thirst for righteousness, for they will be filled."
>
> MATTHEW 5:6 NRSV

What is your usual response when you are hungry? Do you become frustrated or angry? Do you feel like you don't have energy for any of the things you are doing? We need food to nourish us and to keep us going during the day.

In the same way, we need spiritual food that encourages us to keep going in hard times. Take some time to read the Bible, pray with someone else who enjoys praying, or listen to some music and allow the Holy Spirit to speak to you. Find a way to encourage someone who might need to nourish their body or soul.

ACT OF KINDNESS

Bring a neighbor a batch of cookies or treats.

Bad Days

Get rid of all bitterness, rage, anger, harsh words, and slander, as well as all types of evil behavior.

EPHESIANS 4:31 NLT

Everyone has bad days. It might be that your parent's car broke down on the way to school or you couldn't find your rain jacket. Maybe you got angry at someone in your house, or at school, and you haven't felt settled the rest of the day. We can spend the whole day thinking about things that have gone wrong and it can affect everything else we are doing, including how we treat others.

If your day hasn't gone so well, take a moment to ask for wisdom. You might not be able to fix everything in a second, but God can help you get to the other side. If you know someone who has had a bad day, remind them that God will be there whenever they need him.

ACT OF KINDNESS

Compliment the first three people you see today.

Living in Harmony

> In every relationship be swift to choose peace over competition, and run swiftly toward holiness, for those who are not holy will not see the Lord.
>
> HEBREWS 12:14 TPT

The people closest to us are usually the ones who hear all of our complaints and arguments. We can be difficult to live with sometimes, and we just have to admit that! Our family members can also make us feel bad with their comments. Remember that these are the people who will usually love you no matter what.

Make today one where you show nothing but love, grace, and kindness toward the people in your home. Stop complaining, stop whining, and see what change in atmosphere you can bring.

ACT OF KINDNESS

Choose to not argue when someone is upset with you.

Constant and Change

While the earth remains, seedtime and harvest, cold and heat, summer and winter, day and night, shall not cease.

GENESIS 8:22 ESV

The seasons are a great reminder that even though things around us might change, there are still many that stay the same. We know that summer will always arrive. Even though leaves may begin to fall in the autumn, we know they will come back.

This is true of our lives as well. You might feel as though many things in your life are hard. Maybe you need to fix a broken friendship, or you are moving to a new house. These things can be unsettling, and you could be feeling sad or angry. Find hope today by remembering the seasons. Winter might be on its way, but enjoy what you can during this time, and be filled with hope for the start of spring.

ACT OF KINDNESS

Drop off uncarved pumpkins at a family's doorstep.

Going Away

> The Lord gives his people strength.
> The Lord blesses them with peace.
>
> PSALM 29:11 NLT

Vacations can be an amazing way of stopping everything else and enjoying time with your family. Even if you can't go away somewhere nice, you can still have fun just doing something different than normal.

It is good to spend some time on your family relationships. Jesus needed some time away from people and he would often go to a quiet place to rest. Perhaps you can go find Jesus in that restful place and allow him to fill you up with hope and love.

ACT OF KINDNESS

Offer to babysit a child for tired parents.

Decision Maker

Pour out all your worries and stress upon him and leave
them there, for he always tenderly cares for you.

1 PETER 5:7 TPT

Decisions are hard to make. We can get stuck thinking too
much about what we should do. We might write down the
good and bad things that could happen with each choice.
Sometimes it's hard to tell if we aren't sure because we are
afraid to start or because it's wise to wait.

If you are facing a big decision right now, give your worries
and cares to Jesus. When you let him be in control, you
will have the peace you need. You will know that you have
done the right thing when you feel that peace about your
decision. God cares for you, so trust that he will lead you to
the right place.

ACT OF KINDNESS

*Ask a parent if you can buy coffee for
the person in line behind you.*

Proud Of You

I run straight for the divine invitation of reaching the heavenly goal and gaining the victory-prize through the anointing of Jesus.

PHILIPPIANS 3:14 TPT

Do you remember how it felt when you brought home good grades from school or did really well in a game? If you were fortunate enough to grow up in a home where parents would take notice of these things, you will know how good it feels to hear your parents say they are proud of you.

Jesus is proud of you right now whether you bring home a good report card or not. He thinks that you are the best, and no amount of your own self-doubt will change his mind about how wonderful you are. Instead of competing with others to be first or focusing only on your achievements, let someone else win or put someone else before you. What really matters is your kindness.

ACT OF KINDNESS

Let someone go before you in line.

seeking answers

> "You will seek me and find me
> when you seek me with all your heart."
>
> JEREMIAH 29:13 NIV

What are you asking God for right now? If you don't feel like you are getting answers, remember that God is always listening, and he always answers. It just might not be in the way you are expecting. Look for the Holy Spirit in the words of a wise friend, through the Bible, or talking with your parents. Trust that he is guiding you toward the very thing you are seeking.

If you know someone close to you is really searching for answers, give them an encouraging Scripture or let them know that you are praying for them to hear clearly from God as well.

ACT OF KINDNESS

*Pray for a friend who is in the middle
of a difficult situation.*

Exercising Control

If you live without restraint
and are unable to control your temper,
you're as helpless as a city with
broken-down defenses, open to attack.

PROVERBS 25:28 TPT

Do you sometimes catch yourself getting angry, knowing that what you're saying isn't right, but you still let yourself say it anyway? Having an outburst can let out a lot of frustration, but it can also hurt someone you care about. It's important to bring Jesus into your day. Talk to him from morning to evening, so you are aware of his presence and his ability to help you control your emotions.

If you feel like you have been at the other end of someone's unkind words, pray that the Holy Spirit will work on their heart, so they are able to see when they have been unkind. Show them the grace of Jesus by your kind words.

ACT OF KINDNESS

Keep your mouth free from harsh words today.

Restoration

Jesus left Capernaum and went down to the region of Judea and into the area east of the Jordan River. Once again crowds gathered around him, and as usual he was teaching them.

MARK 10:1 NLT

When Jesus was followed by large groups of people asking him to help them, to heal them, to teach them, and to save them, he must have gotten tired of the requests. But the Bible says that he was able to take the weight of the world on his shoulders.

As you look around your world today you will see a lot of people who are suffering, and you may feel as though it is just too much for God to deal with. But God is far greater, far more powerful, and far smarter than we can even understand. Instead of losing hope over this world, have hope that Jesus is continuing to bring restoration through us.

ACT OF KINDNESS

Pray for someone who is hurting.

Love Instruction

Those who love your instructions
have great peace and do not stumble.

PSALM 119:165 NLT

We are know what stress is. There are so many things in our life that cause us to be worried, pressured, and anxious. The world presents us with situations that steal our joy and take our peace. You might be facing some of those situations today.

Spend time with God and let his peace wash over your heart. Focus on his truth rather than your problems. God can take everything that is troubling you today and exchange it for peace.

ACT OF KINDNESS

Pick flowers for someone at home.

Burned

> Put on God's complete set of armor provided for us,
> so that you will be protected as you fight
> against the evil strategies of the accuser!
>
> EPHESIANS 6:11 TPT

Have you ever looked in the mirror at the end of a long day outside and realized that you got more sun than you thought? Now your skin is red, or your tan lines are really obvious. Sometimes we forget to take the precautions we need when we go into the world. We don't put on our spiritual armor to guard us from the attacks of the enemy. You might get home and realize that you have been burned by what has gone on in your day.

Make sure that you put on the full armor of God when you head out into the world, so you are equipped to handle what might come your way. Be ready to defend someone else if they look like they are under some kind of attack as well.

ACT OF KINDNESS

Include someone in a conversation who usually doesn't have much to say.

meaningful affection

He touched their eyes. He said,
"It will happen to you just as you believed."

MATTHEW 9:29 NIRV

There will be people in your life who really love hugs. Their love language is human touch. You might not be someone who likes to give or even receive that kind of affection, but it's important to understand that everyone loves in different ways.

If there's someone in your life today who you know is struggling or just needs a little pick me up, spend some time with them and make sure to give them a hug or a pat on the shoulder. These small things show them that you really care for them. Just like Jesus, our touch can bring healing to someone's mind and heart.

ACT OF KINDNESS

Give someone a hug.

In the Light

> You are a chosen race, a royal priesthood,
> a holy nation, a people for his own possession,
> that you may proclaim the excellencies of him
> who called you out of darkness into his marvelous light.
>
> 1 PETER 2:9 ESV

Nighttime can be scary because we can't see what is going on. The same slam of a car door in the day doesn't concern you like it does when you hear it at night. Loud voices on the street at night make you more nervous than in the day.

This is just like the experience of life without the light of Jesus. People are anxious and fearful, unsure of their future. When the light of Jesus shines and gives people a reason to hope, people can walk in confidence. If there's a way you can bring light into someone's life today, find it!

ACT OF KINDNESS

Read a story to someone before bed.

My Portion Forever

My body and my heart may grow weak.
God, you give strength to my heart.
You are everything I will ever need.

PSALM 73:26 NIRV

There are times when we feel strong and independent and there are times when we realize that we need others. God gave us gifts and strengths, but we are still not perfect. At times, we just have to admit that we can't do it all on our own.

God is the source of strength. There is great peace in knowing that God is our rock, now and forever. When control is lost and fear is present, there is one thing we can know for certain. He is our strength; he never loses control. Imitate Jesus and be that rock to someone who is sick or heartbroken today.

ACT OF KINDNESS

Send a Scripture text to a friend.

No Words

Let the words of my mouth
and the meditation of my heart
be acceptable to you, O Lord,
my rock and my redeemer.

PSALM 19:14 NRSV

When people are going through difficult times, they often ask others for advice. Sometimes we don't know how to respond because we don't have the answers or wisdom to help. You might be worried about what you will say when you are having a tough discussion with someone. You might want to bring your faith into the conversation but just don't know how that person will receive it.

Remember that the Holy Spirit is your helper. You have the most wise and loving person at your side, and he can fill you with the right words. Even if you don't get your words exactly right, his love will still shine through you.

ACT OF KINDNESS

Send a positive text message to five different people.

Stuck in the Mud

Our struggle is not against flesh and blood,
but against the rulers, against the authorities,
against the powers of this dark world and against
the spiritual forces of evil in the heavenly realms.

EPHESIANS 6:12 NIV

Have you ever been walking through mud and found that you have to walk slowly and carefully so you don't get your shoes stuck as you take the next step? Life can be a bit like this sometimes. You might feel like it is too hard to take another step. You might not have the strength to move ahead.

If you feel like you are in this position right now, ask for help. Jesus doesn't want you to be weighed down by sin or other circumstances. Be ready for his help and trust that he will bring you freedom. Get ready to start running again.

ACT OF KINDNESS

Go for a walk with a family member or friend.

Outward Looking

Pray in the Spirit at all times with all kinds of prayers, asking for everything you need. To do this you must always be ready and never give up. Always pray for all God's people.

EPHESIANS 6:18 NCV

It can be hard to know the needs of others around you. You might not know how a friend is feeling or how someone from church is doing. You might be so focused on yourself that you have forgotten about the homeless people in the cities or the people in other parts of the world who are suffering from many different things.

Think outside of your space to the community around you and see if there are ways that you can extend your generosity to those who need it the most.

ACT OF KINDNESS

Pray for someone in need.

Supporting Leaders

Be careful to live properly among your unbelieving neighbors. Then even if they accuse you of doing wrong, they will see your honorable behavior, and they will give honor to God when he judges the world.

1 Peter 2:12-14 NLT

Our leaders and decision-makers are not perfect. We might only hear the worst about the people in power, but we also need to recognize that God can work in their hearts, and they need the grace of Jesus as much as we do.

Pray for your leaders. You don't have to agree with them, but you can honor them by asking God to grant them more integrity and help them lead more wisely.

ACT OF KINDNESS

Send a thank-you card to a leader.

comfort in the Promise

> Your promise revives me;
> it comforts me in all my troubles.
>
> PSALM 119:50 NLT

Grief is strange. It shows up in weird places. We can smile, we can laugh, and we can be perfectly happy, but the pain of grief is still there deep down. We don't forget it, but we shouldn't feel bad about smiling either.

As a child of God, you have been promised a hope that has the power to give you life even in tough moments. Though your pain is real and deep, God is strong and able to lift you out of the deepest pit and—even when it's hard to imagine—give you joy.

ACT OF KINDNESS

Share a joyful memory with your family.

Living the Future

Surely goodness and mercy
shall follow me all the days of my life,
and I shall dwell in the house of the LORD
my whole life long.

PSALM 23:6 NRSV

Are you someone who dreams about your future, or do you who take each day as it comes? If you always look ahead or make sure you achieve things every day, remember that God is in each of your steps. Jesus is right beside you, leading you toward a bright future of green pastures.

Let yourself be hopeful for the future, but also think about those who are struggling to survive, who don't know what tomorrow will look like. Pray for them and do something today that will help them understand God's help in their life.

ACT OF KINDNESS

Put a positive note in your neighbor's mailbox.

NOVEMBER

Love each other with genuine affection,
and take delight in honoring each other.

ROMANS 12:10 NLT

Why Not

"Call to me and I will answer you
and tell you great and unsearchable things
you do not know."

JEREMIAH 33:3 NIV

While it may seem like your parents say no a lot, they do it mostly out of love. They say no because they don't want a child to get hurt, or because that child might be about to hurt someone else. Sometimes they say no because they can't do what you are asking them to do.

You might be praying for something and feel like God is saying no. Be encouraged that God is listening to you and that he is looking at what is the best for you. If he says no, you can be sure it is for a good reason.

ACT OF KINDNESS

Donate toys to your church.

Perfect Weather

> Those who wait for perfect weather
> will never plant seeds; those who look at
> every cloud will never harvest crops.
>
> ECCLESIASTES 11:4 NCV

If you live in a place that has a lot of different weather, your parents probably spend time watching your weather report. This might be necessary if they are trying to make decisions about events or day trips or what work they might be able to do on the house.

Instead of spending your time worrying about the weather, let yourself enjoy whatever is happening. Take the opportunities that come with the different seasons. Go for a walk if it's sunny, fly a kite if it's windy, and build a snowman if it snows. Make the weather your friend!

ACT OF KINDNESS

Do something outside with a friend.

Led by Compassion

> Peter said, "Silver or gold I do not have,
> but what I do have I give you. In the name of
> Jesus Christ of Nazareth, walk."
>
> ACTS 3:6 NIV

You might get tired of seeing people shake buckets at you as you enter a grocery store. It can seem we are always asked to give and give some more. The story of the beggar at the gates in the Bible is a beautiful picture of responding to someone's needs that might go beyond money.

When Peter and John were walking by, the beggar asked for money. Even though they didn't have the money, they had the power of God. The beggar went from having nothing to being completely healed! Jesus can work miracles through you too. You might just have to be willing to stop and think about what you have to offer.

ACT OF KINDNESS

Offer to pray for someone who is sick.

skyscrapers

Great is your love. It reaches to the heavens.
Your truth reaches to the skies.

PSALM 57:10 NIRV

Have you ever seen anything come close to reaching the heavens? The tallest tree might look spectacular, and the highest skyscraper appears amazing, but these things are nothing in comparison to the mercy of God!

It is part of our nature to look at other people's behaviors and attitudes and compare them to our own. When you feel like you might be doing that, let God's mercy help you to look at things differently. His love is so much greater than our complaints.

ACT OF KINDNESS

Send a nice note to a friend.

I'm Bored

Besides that, they learn to waste their time, going from house to house. And they not only waste their time but also begin to gossip and busy themselves with other people's lives, saying things they should not say.

1 TIMOTHY 5:13 NCV

Kids usually complain about boredom because they do not have the same responsibilities as adults. When your parents hear, "I have nothing to do!" it can seem crazy. They would probably love to have nothing to do for a little while.

The Bible says that boredom can lead us to make bad choices. Stay active so you don't fall into trouble by yourself or with your friends. Find something to do that helps others when you are feeling bored.

ACT OF KINDNESS

Ask your parents how you can help them.

paper planes

> All Scripture is inspired by God and is useful to teach us what is true and to make us realize what is wrong in our lives. It corrects us when we are wrong and teaches us to do what is right.
>
> 2 TIMOTHY 3:16 NLT

If you've ever tried to make a paper plane that is fancy, you'll know you have to follow some complicated instructions. If you don't follow each fold carefully, your plane will wobble and not fly very far.

The Bible is our instruction guide; it gives us the right way to live. If we make sure we follow the instructions, it will help us to soar, and we will be much better for it. If you feel someone could benefit from the wisdom of Scripture, find a gentle way to suggest it.

ACT OF KINDNESS

Write a kind message on a mirror or whiteboard.

Thank You

"Oh, thank you, sir!" she exclaimed.
Then she went back and began to eat again,
and she was no longer sad.

1 SAMUEL 25:33 NLT

When people do kind things for us it can change our attitudes from sad to happy. When was the last time someone did something nice for you? When was the last time you did something good for someone else?

Whether you have received or given, it is always nice to know that it has been appreciated. Taking the extra effort to say thank you is always worth it. It's good to acknowledge goodness and have hearts full of gratitude.

ACT OF KINDNESS

*Send a thank-you card to your
local police or fire station.*

Heart over Knowledge

To do righteousness and justice is more acceptable to the LORD than sacrifice.

PROVERBS 21:3 NRSV

We study hard for tests because good grades prove we have what we need to continue our education. If we get the right grades, it means we can go to college. Because we talk so much about earning things, we often try to prove our knowledge about the things of God so we can be accepted by him. This is not how God sees things.

God knows that if we love him and love others, then we have already passed the test! It is about your heart and your willingness to love the world around you that matters the most.

ACT OF KINDNESS

Write a quick note to a teacher.

Simple Strength

> God gives me strength for the battle.
> He keeps my way secure.
>
> PSALM 18:32 NIRV

Have you ever had a hard time coming up with the right words to explain yourself? We don't always have all the answers and sometimes we just need to admit that we don't get it. This verse is a good reminder that God is the source of our strength.

When you are going through a difficult time, or have a tough decision to make, you don't have to decide on your own. Instead ask God and the people he has put in your life to help you like your parents. They will guide your mind and your heart toward the right thing.

ACT OF KINDNESS

Call someone you love just to say, "I love you."

fearless confidence

> The one who walks in integrity will experience a
> fearless confidence in life, but the one who
> is devious will eventually be exposed.
>
> PROVERBS 10:9 TPT

Integrity is doing the right thing even when knows. It is so important for your study, work, and relationships. People need to be able to trust you, and they will give you more important things to do when you prove that you are able to be trusted. With Jesus in your life, you can be sure that he is always with you.

Sometimes we need to be reminded that our actions are seen by him. Take some time to think about what you have been doing today and if you would do it the same way standing next to Jesus. If you need to ask for forgiveness, ask! Then make sure you do the right thing next time.

ACT OF KINDNESS

Complete a task you said you would do for someone.

Fighting for You

> God is our refuge and strength,
> a very present help in trouble.
> Therefore we will not fear,
> though the earth should change,
> though the mountains shake in the heart of the sea;
> though its waters roar and foam,
> though the mountains tremble with its tumult.
>
> PSALM 46:1-3 NRSV

What troubles and fears are you facing right now? Are you worried if you will have enough time to study for a test? God is our help when we need it the most. Sometimes we need more than just help for our minds and hearts. Sometimes we need food or protection. God can help us through others, and often that's the way God shows up.

Have you experienced kindness, generosity, or protection from someone recently? Thank God for being your help in times of trouble.

ACT OF KINDNESS

*Say thank you to an active military member
or veteran today.*

Turning Away

God is faithful and fair. If we confess our sins,
he will forgive our sins. He will forgive every wrong
thing we have done. He will make us pure.

1 JOHN 1:9 NIRV

Repentance isn't just about praying the right prayer and
saying the right words. It is an act of turning away from the
sin that you have been caught in. You might need to turn
away over and over again to keep your heart clean before
God. It doesn't mean you will always do things right but it
does mean that you are doing your best.

Be encouraged that Jesus' grace covers all sin; there is
nothing you are not forgiven of. If you see someone who
is tangled up in sin, pray that they will find the power of
Jesus to turn away from it.

ACT OF KINDNESS

Ask for forgiveness from someone you have wronged.

An Excellent Spirit

This Daniel became distinguished above all
the other high officials and satraps,
because an excellent spirit was in him.
And the king planned to set him
over the whole kingdom.

DANIEL 6:3 ESV

What have you grown in lately? You might have finished a project ahead of schedule, had a small win in a sport, or you may have passed a test with great grades. Well done!

As you think about what you have been able to do, remember who it is that has given you the skills, talents, and gifts to make is possible. You are blessed and it is good to say with humility that the Lord created you to do good things.

ACT OF KINDNESS

Offer to help teach your talent to a younger child.

Restored and Revived

That's where he restores and revives my life.
He opens before me pathways to God's pleasure
and leads me along in his footsteps of righteousness
so that I can bring honor to his name.

PSALMS 23:3 TPT

When the good shepherd guides you to green pastures, you will be restored. You need to rest and know that he will provide for you. What have you seen God open up in front of you?

As you let God lead you on a journey of faith, trust that each step he offers you to take with him is right. Don't be led by anxiety; allow him to bring you into a place of peace. Stop and let him give you life, so you can trust him in your next decision.

ACT OF KINDNESS

Help someone rake their leaves.

Automation

Whatever you do, work at it with all your heart,
as working for the Lord, not for human masters.

COLOSSIANS 3:23 NIV

Most things we do now are digital. We can command things to turn on with our voice and ask for directions from our phones without having to lift a finger. While automation has its benefits, we also need to be aware that it can make us less willing to put in the hard work when we need to.

Doing kind things for others will often require some effort. You might have to give up some of your time to help someone. That can't be done with the push of a button. Ask God to give you the strength and desire to be generous.

ACT OF KINDNESS

*Ask an elderly neighbor if you can
help them with something.*

Last Minute

"Take what belongs to you and go. I choose to give to this last worker as I give to you."

MATTHEW 20:14 ESV

Today is the day! You might be very good at waiting until the very last minute to do something like those who give their hearts to Jesus at the end of their life. But the point of the parable Jesus told in the verse above was that we are more blessed to live in the freedom, peace, and joy of walking with Christ during our whole lives.

It is better to live with Jesus and share his hope with those around you now. Share your faith with honesty and bravery, knowing it is much better not to leave it to the last minute.

ACT OF KINDNESS

Share a Scripture of hope with someone.

Windy Words

I have heard many such things;
miserable comforters are you all.
Have windy words no limit?
Or what provokes you that you keep on talking?

JOB 16:2-3 NRSV

Job suffered a lot. Everything was taken from him including his health. Although he had friends to visit and keep him company, they clearly were not able to say the right thing! Each of these friends had their turn at offering advice. What he really needed was wise people to just sit and listen.

If you know of someone who is suffering, ask the Holy Spirit how you can help them best. It could be just to sit with them and let them know they are not alone. Hold back your opinions. Be sensitive and aware of what God is doing before you speak.

ACT OF KINDNESS

Be a listening ear for a friend in need.

Breath of God

The earth was without form and void, and darkness was over the face of the deep. And the Spirit of God was hovering over the face of the waters.

GENESIS 1:2 ESV

The word for the Holy Spirit in this verse, *ruach*, can mean wind, breath, or spirit. The Spirit that was hovering over the waters in the beginning is the same Spirit that lives in you. You might not think you are very spiritual if you compare yourself to others who pray, go to church, or read the Bible more than you, but you have the Spirit of God in you!

You don't have to be religious or perfect at every spiritual discipline, just let the Holy Spirit in you turn the ordinary into something extraordinary.

ACT OF KINDNESS

Offer to help out at church this week.

Wisdom as a Person

Give instruction to the wise,
and they will become wiser still;
teach the righteous and
they will gain in learning.

PROVERBS 9:9 NRSV

This verse isn't suggesting that you have to be smart to be taught. It means that you are smart simply by accepting that you need to be taught. Are there times when you have sat in a classroom thinking negatively about everything your teacher has to say? Maybe you start to roll your eyes when an older person begins telling you what they think.

You don't have to listen to everything people say, but it is good to ask for wisdom from people you trust. God has put people in your life to help guide you into what is best for you. Be teachable.

ACT OF KINDNESS

*Call a grandparent and tell them
how much you love them.*

The Animal Kingdom

> Good people take care of their animals,
> but even the kindest acts of the wicked are cruel.
>
> PROVERBS 12:10 NCV

Have you ever been encouraged by an animal? It might be a sweet song of a bird or a cat crawling onto your lap. Maybe it was a look from a dog or the gentle hum of a hummingbird. The animal kingdom is an incredible part of God's creation. He can use them to bring joy, help, and comfort to us.

What is your favorite animal? Do you have one? When you think of that creature, thank God for his incredible handiwork.

ACT OF KINDNESS

Feed the birds.

marriage

"The two will become one flesh.
So they are no longer two, but one flesh."

MARK 10:8 NIV

Many marriages do not work out. This is sad, and we are still shocked when people separate. Temptation and stress can lead people in different directions. Maybe you have experienced the separation of your parents or another breakup in your family. This is a difficult thing to walk through.

We all have different journeys, and we never know how they will work out, but we can trust that God works all things together for good for those who trust in his ways. Pray today for a marriage in your family and ask God to make it strong.

ACT OF KINDNESS

*Help a married couple with their kids
so they can spend time together.*

Without Worrying

Anxiety in a man's heart weighs him down,
but a good word makes him glad.

PROVERBS 12:25 ESV

We spend a lot of time waiting for good things. Have you ever wanted to be older so you could do the same things older kids can do? Maybe you can't wait for your birthday or Christmas because you love celebrations so much.

We wait for other things too. In a checkout line. For the bus. To get our grades back. In times of waiting, it does no good to worry about things we can't control. Try to be thankful for what you are doing now and trust for the best. You can't control what happens, but you can control how patient you are when you have to wait.

ACT OF KINDNESS

Go for a walk with a friend or family member.

Generosity from Afar

"You must go and make disciples of all nations.
Baptize them in the name of the Father
and of the Son and of the Holy Spirit."

MATTHEW 28:19 NIRV

Are there certain countries you want to visit? What is it about those places that makes you want to go there? Is it the beauty of the landscape or the culture? You may just want to be in a place different than where you are right now.

Take some time to think about the people in the place you want to visit and consider what they might be going through. Focus your thoughts and prayers on those in need. Remember that Jesus wanted the gospel to be preached to the ends of the earth so do your part and send his light and love to someone on the other side of the world.

ACT OF KINDNESS

Pray for children in another country.

Slow Burn

The LORD is compassionate and gracious,
slow to anger, abounding in love.

PSALM 103:8 NIV

What do you want to get done today? We wake up and have a lot of things to do even before we head out the door! Sometimes in our rush, we can get irritable and unkind especially when things don't go smoothly. This makes us feel rushed and we get angry quickly.

It might help to know that God is not like this at all! His nature is love first and love always. This means that he is slow to anger and really, really quick to accept you even if you're in a bad mood. Think about how much grace God has for you and let this inspire you to be more gracious to others.

ACT OF KINDNESS

Make breakfast for someone.

Perfectly Imperfect

> We all stumble in many ways. And if anyone does not stumble in what he says, he is a perfect man, able also to bridle his whole body.
>
> JAMES 3:2 ESV

When children do jobs for their parents, the job isn't usually done perfectly, but a parent is filled with joy when their children are proud of completing a task. If the child does the chore happily and without being told to, it is even more celebrated by the parent.

We can't expect to do all of God's work perfectly and he doesn't need us to. He just wants us to help be a part of his work on earth. Try new things even if you might not do them well the first or second time. It will always be your heart attitude that matters.

ACT OF KINDNESS

Make someone's bed for them.

Faith Explanation

> I am not ashamed of this Good News about Christ.
> It is the power of God at work, saving everyone who
> believes—the Jew first and also the Gentile.
>
> ROMANS 1:16 NLT

It can feel strange to be a Christian. People believe different things, and it can be confusing. Although friends may not tease you for your faith, many believe there is not only one right way. Some don't even want to know if there is right and wrong. Instead of fighting, try to explain your faith in a different way.

No one can argue with your personal relationship with Jesus. They can see your peace even if they don't want to admit it. If you get a chance this week to mention your faith, be brave and share the gospel that has freed you and can free others.

ACT OF KINDNESS

Bring treats to a neighbor or friend.

Ripple Effect

> The Lord said, "Your strength will not get my temple rebuilt. Your power will not do it either. Only the power of my Spirit will do it," says the Lord who rules over all.
>
> ZECHARIAH 4:6 NIRV

When you throw a rock into still water, it will probably disappear from sight, but you know it has been there because you see the ripples that start at the point the rock went into the water. The circles start small and then get bigger and bigger as they move out. The effect of the ripples is much greater than the size of the actual rock.

In the same way, Jesus can use our acts of kindness for something greater than we see. What could you do today that might seem small to you but will move into the community around you? Trust that God will keep using your gift for good. Just start with a brave act and then let God take over.

ACT OF KINDNESS

Say something kind about someone to someone else.

Warning Signs

Do not regard them as enemies,
but warn them as believers.

2 Thessalonians 3:15 NRSV

For every warning there is a reason. It could be a sign to tell you something is wet so you don't slip. It could be a siren from an ambulance saying you need to move out of its way. Even a quick on your tongue tells you the food is too hot. Warnings can help us make better decisions.

You might feel anxious after making a decision, and sometimes that makes you want to change your mind. Spiritual warnings keep us from harm or keep us from hurting others. Pay close attention to the Holy Spirit and what he might be guiding you to stay away from. Trust that God cares about you and your decisions.

ACT OF KINDNESS

*Thank a friend who has helped you
make good decisions.*

In His Image

> Then God said, "Let us make man in our image, after our likeness. And let them have dominion over the fish of the sea and over the birds of the heavens and over the livestock and over all the earth and over every creeping thing that creeps on the earth."
>
> GENESIS 1:26 ESV

God created you in his image. Have you ever thought about what this really means? God wants his followers to show the rest of the world what he is like. He wants us to tell them about his wonderful creation and his faithfulness to us.

That might seem like a big task! But showing Jesus to other people isn't just something you do, it's who you are. Be encouraged today that you are showing your Creator to others just by being you.

ACT OF KINDNESS

Send someone a text telling them they are beautiful.

BUT I SAY

"You have heard the law that says, 'Love your neighbor' and hate your enemy. But I say, love your enemies! Pray for those who persecute you!"

MATTHEW 5:43-44 NLT

The ways of the world are different than the ways of God's kingdom. Jesus made this clear by showing the difference between how the world treats their enemies and how we are supposed to treat them. You probably have people in your life that are unkind toward you. Sometimes we even get teased about our faith. These are the very people Jesus asks us to love.

It's not easy to pray for those who hurt you. Jesus understands this. He had to forgive all of us for all of our sin. Let him be your strength as you practice goodness to those who have hurt you.

ACT OF KINDNESS

Be kind to someone who isn't kind to you.

DECEMBER

Our love can't be an abstract theory
we only talk about, but a way of life
demonstrated through our loving deeds.

1 John 3:18 tpt

A Big Task

"Now Israel's cry for help has reached me. I have seen how badly the Egyptians are treating them. So now, go. I am sending you to Pharaoh. I want you to bring the Israelites out of Egypt. They are my people."

EXODUS 3:9-10 NIRV

Have you ever felt like God gave you a job that was too big for you to handle? After Moses had seen God in the burning bush, he was asked to take the people of Israel out of the land of Egypt and away from Pharaoh. This was going to be an amazing victory for the Israelites, but it required a huge amount of effort from Moses.

What has God asked you to do today, this week, or this year? Does it feel like it is too big for you? God wants to do amazing things through you, and he will give you everything you need to do it if you ask.

ACT OF KINDNESS

Help your parents out around the house.

speak well

> "I hope I continue to please you, sir," she replied. "You have comforted me by speaking so kindly to me, even though I am not one of your workers."
>
> RUTH 2:13 NLT

It's hard to feel good about yourself in a world where everyone compares themselves to others. While we don't want to waste our skills and talents, we also don't want to focus on using them to show that we are the best at something. We want to use them to help others!

We should be encouraging people who are doing well because they are using their gifts to help make the world a better place. Think of someone you admire and praise them for what they do really well.

ACT OF KINDNESS

Tell someone how good they are at something.

Give It Up

Calling the crowd to join his disciples, he said, "If any of you wants to be my follower, you must give up your own way, take up your cross, and follow me."

MARK 8:34 NLT

We get up in the morning with good ideas about how to spend our day. We want to work hard, be kind, and help others. Sometimes we succeed, but many times we don't. We want to follow Jesus, but he asks us to follow him his way, and that can be hard to do.

As you start your day, commit your ways to God's ways, and surrender your desires to his. Trust him to lead you on the right path. He knows what is best!

ACT OF KINDNESS

Take out the trash for your parents.

Servant of All

He sat down, called the twelve,
and said to them, "Whoever wants to be first
must be last of all and servant of all."

MARK 9:35 NRSV

The disciples were talking about who would be greater in God's kingdom, and Jesus had to remind them that his kingdom doesn't work like the world's. Jesus tells his friends that being first in this life doesn't count for much in heaven.

To be great in God's kingdom means loving others first. It's not about rising to the top above others. Think about this today and choose kindness instead of selfishness.

ACT OF KINDNESS

Give a household member a shoulder massage.

Let Them Come

> People were bringing little children to Jesus for him to place his hands on them, but the disciples rebuked them. When Jesus saw this, he was indignant. He said to them, "Let the little children come to me, and do not hinder them, for the kingdom of God belongs to such as these."
>
> MARK 10:13-14 NIV

Does your life feel busy? Sometimes you don't pay attention to the little things because big things are taking up your time. Where do you spend the most time, and do you think it is the best use of your time?

The disciples thought that Jesus' teaching was more important than the children, but Jesus told them to bring the children to him. Jesus loves those who need him. Have a heart that wants to be with him. Find time to do those small but important things today.

ACT OF KINDNESS

Help a mom with her small children.

Bless the Poor

Jesus turned to his disciples and said, "God blesses you who are poor, for the Kingdom of God is yours."

LUKE 6:20 NLT

It doesn't matter whether you have money or not, you can be poor in many ways. Maybe you don't have a really close friend, and you feel lonely. Maybe things are hard for your family right now, and you feel sad.

When we feel this way, God reminds us that he will bless us. Life will have ups and downs, but God wants you to experience his goodness. He wants you to know that he will take care of everything you need. Find a way to share this hope with someone who is feeling sad.

ACT OF KINDNESS

Spend time with a friend or family member.

Overloaded

> Jesus said, "Come to me, all of you who are weary and carry heavy burdens, and I will give you rest."
>
> MATTHEW 11:28 NLT

Have you ever been with someone who went into a grocery store to get a few things but ended up grabbing a lot more? They probably didn't grab a shopping cart and were trying to balance everything on top of each other, hoping they could make it to the checkout without dropping something.

When we have a lot of different things going on, sometimes it can feel like we are losing control. We might get more upset at our families than normal, or feel anxious, or not be able to focus on one thing at a time. Sometimes we need to look at everything we are doing and decide that some things just need to wait. Stop and ask Jesus if he can carry some of the heavy stuff for you.

ACT OF KINDNESS

Help someone carry something.

LOOK at Me

Let your eyes look straight ahead;
fix your gaze directly before you.

PROVERBS 4:25 NIV

We all probably spend too much time on our phones.
It's easy to do. We use them for information, videos, and
communication. Even if our phones are very helpful, they
can cause problems when we are spending time with
people. If we look at our phones when people are talking
to us, those people think we don't care about what they
have to say.

Think about how you feel when you are with other people,
and make sure you do for them what you would want them
to do for you. Set your phone aside. Be more like Jesus as
you listen and care for others.

ACT OF KINDNESS

*Put your phone away when you're
spending time with someone.*

The Hand Dealt

I saw that under the sun the race is not to the swift,
nor the battle to the strong,
nor bread to the wise,
nor riches to the intelligent,
nor favor to those with knowledge,
but time and chance happen to them all.

ECCLESIASTES 9:11 ESV

Most card games include both skill and luck. You are dealt certain cards and then you have to decide how you can try to win. Sometimes you just don't have all the right cards. In the same way, you might have been given a difficult situation to grow up in. You have to work with what you've been given, but God's grace is there for you every step of the way.

Let the gentle guiding of the Holy Spirit and the wisdom of older people you trust help you to find your way through the hard and easy days. Be kind to someone today who you know is having a hard time.

ACT OF KINDNESS

Donate gently used jackets to your school.

Rainstorm

Poor people have come to you for safety.
You have kept needy people safe
when they were in trouble.
You have been a place to hide when storms came.
You have been a shade from the heat of the sun.
Evil people attack us.
They are like a storm beating against a wall.

ISAIAH 25:4 NIRV

Distractions come in many forms. They can be notifications on your phone, requests from a friend, or a hunger pain in your stomach. Distractions stop us from getting things done, and they stop us from paying attention to things we need to pay attention to.

What is distracting you right now? What is God trying to get your attention about? Sometimes we don't want to ask him because we are afraid of the answer. Trust that he wants what is best for you.

ACT OF KINDNESS

Check something off your list of things to do.

Two Are Better

Two people are better off than one,
for they can help each other succeed.

ECCLESIASTES 4:9 NLT

Part of becoming close to people is having meals together.
A lot can be shared over the dinner table or even over
a cup of coffee. Think of someone you feel comfortable
doing this with. Often they are the people who are closest
to you.

How would you feel if the people closest to you turned
against you? Sometimes our relationships with people fall
apart. When that happens, we need Jesus to step in. If you
are grieving over a lost friendship, bring it to the Lord in
prayer.

ACT OF KINDNESS

Invite a friend over for lunch or dinner.

Flowing from Goodness

Everything you do is beautiful,
flowing from your goodness;
teach me the power of
your wonderful words!

PSALM 119:68 TPT

You will probably smile as you greet the people you come across today; you might smile as you say goodbye to your loved ones for the day. You might even share a few laughs with friends or the people you go to school with.

We don't give much thought to a smile, but it's a really powerful sign that can cheer someone up in an instant. If no one has smiled at you yet this morning, be the person who smiles first. Bring cheer to someone else's day by your happy heart and wonderful words.

ACT OF KINDNESS

Smile at everyone you see today.

AS I LOVE

> "My command is this: Love each other
> as I have loved you."
>
> JOHN 15:12 NIV

Do you know what it means to pay it forward? You do a kind act for someone, and they pass that kindness on to another person, and so it continues—kind act after kind act, spreading goodness to people all over the world. This is the fruit described in the Bible.

What we do here, in the name of God, lasts forever. Any goodness we do for God is going to make fruit. That fruit will shed seeds that will be planted somewhere else in the name of God, blessing person after person.

ACT OF KINDNESS

Offer to help clean a friend's room.

Overcome With Good

> Do not be overcome by evil,
> but overcome evil with good.
>
> **ROMANS 12:21** NIV

It's not easy to admit when you make a mistake. Sometimes you know as you're saying something that it's not the right thing to say. Sometimes you don't realize until later that you're actually wrong about how you understood a situation.

It's humbling to admit that you have misjudged a person or a situation, but it is equally important to say it out loud. Admit when you are wrong and say sorry. It is rare to hear someone apologize for their mistake, but it goes a long way toward bringing healing to a relationship.

ACT OF KINDNESS

Say sorry to someone you have hurt.

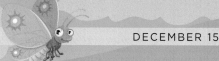

Work Rewards

The Lord is loving.
You reward people for what they have done.

PSALM 62:12 NCV

Sometimes your heart is pulled in many different directions. It isn't always something bad that creates confusion about what to do or where to go, sometimes it is two good things that you have to choose between, and one might not even be more right than the other. It could be a sport choice, which friend gets your attention, or what classes to take next year.

In these times you have to rely on God's faithfulness. He is ready to teach you his ways, but sometimes you have to get it wrong first before you understand about getting it right. Give yourself some grace, and let God keep leading you.

ACT OF KINDNESS

Bring candy canes to your classmates.

Whatever You Do

Whatever you do, do well.
For when you go to the grave,
there will be no work or planning
or knowledge or wisdom.

ECCLESIASTES 9:10 NLT

Trying out for sports or a performance is never fun. You are usually full of nerves about saying the right thing and showing your skill. You might need to be reminded to count your nerves as a blessing because they tell you that you really care about things.

If you are trying something new right now, be brave. God has made you with unique gifts and skills that no other person has. Write down all these gifts and skills so you can present them well. Be encouraged that God thinks you are amazing, and he will find the perfect fit for you.

ACT OF KINDNESS

*Offer to help your coach or teacher
with an extra task.*

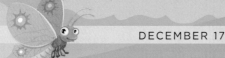

God's Love-gift

Children are God's love-gift;
they are heaven's generous reward.

PSALM 127:3 TPT

A child is at the center of a parent's world. Most good parents don't think about their choices and decisions without thinking about how it will affect their children. Usually they make choices entirely for their children's benefit. A good parent will protect their children at all costs. They will keep them safe and secure.

This is the kind of love God has for you. He is the perfect parent, who is fully for you, and he will protect you. Choose to see God as your perfect parent today.

ACT OF KINDNESS

Say something encouraging to a parent today.

small seeds

> "It is the smallest of all seeds, but when it has grown it is larger than all the garden plants and becomes a tree, so that the birds of the air come and make nests in its branches."
>
> MATTHEW 13:32 ESV

The Lord's riches are found in his goodness, his grace, and his rule as King over everything. God is always able to provide for our needs. Sometimes we might think we are not worthy to receive from God, and sometimes we find it hard to trust him.

The good news of Jesus Christ is that he has given you the ability to talk to God directly. You are a child of the King, and he wants to bless you. All you need to do is love him, ask him, and trust in his goodness. He promises to talk care of you.

ACT OF KINDNESS

Feed the birds.

feast for the poor

"When you give a banquet, invite those who are poor.
Also invite those who can't see or walk. Then you
will be blessed. Your guests can't pay you back.
But you will be paid back when those who are
right with God rise from the dead."

LUKE 14:13-14 NIRV

There might be a lot of things we don't like about church.
But no matter what we think, we need to remember that
God loves the Church. He calls it his bride and he wants her
to help expand his kingdom.

What are some things your church is involved in right now?
Can you give your time and help the good works that your
church has begun? God uses his Church to do amazing
things, so make yourself a willing part of it.

ACT OF KINDNESS

Volunteer at a church event.

Helper

"The Father will send the Friend in my name
to help you. The Friend is the Holy Spirit.
He will teach you all things. He will remind you
of everything I have said to you."

JOHN 14:26 NIRV

It takes a lot of patience to work with children every day.
Teachers have a lot of stress to deal with. Not only are they
trying to teach kids new skills and information, but they are
also dealing with their behavior. This can be very tiring, and
they will need some time alone in order to have the energy
to keep going each day.

Figure out a way that you can appreciate the teachers in
your life today.

ACT OF KINDNESS

Tell a teacher what an amazing job they are doing.

careful words

> "I tell you that on the Judgment Day people will be responsible for every careless thing they have said. The words you have said will be used to judge you. Some of your words will prove you right, but some of your words will prove you guilty."
>
> MATTHEW 12:36-37 NCV

Have you ever heard a group of people start to talk badly about someone you know? Sometimes we like these talks because we don't find that person easy to get along with either and it feels good to have people agree with us. But we only make things worse when we don't walk away from those conversations.

Invite the Holy Spirit into your conversations so you can be aware when they are not good. Think about how you would feel if others were talking about you behind your back and stop the hurtful talk before it gets worse.

ACT OF KINDNESS

Send an encouraging text to someone you know.

Wiser with Age

Older people are wise,
and long life brings understanding.

JOB 12:12 NCV

It is sad that in many cultures older people are not treated with the respect they deserve. There is a lot of wisdom to be learned from people who have walked through life for longer than we have. We would be smart to spend time asking them for helpful life hacks.

Wise people listen to instruction; they continue to look for the best ways to do things. Righteous people want to add to the truth they already know. Is your heart open to learn? Do you want to add to your knowledge of the truth of God's Word? God delights in you chasing after him, and he will teach you how to be wise.

ACT OF KINDNESS

Encourage an older person today with a kind word.

Angelic Faces

"See that you do not despise one of these little ones. For I tell you that in heaven their angels always see the face of my Father who is in heaven."

MATTHEW 18:10 ESV

Our heavenly Father's love is never ending. Think about that for a minute. There is nothing you do to change how he feels about you. It's easy to forget we are already loved perfectly. God loves us more than we can imagine, and he would do anything for us.

Who do you love the most here on earth? What would you do for them? The love you have for that person is a very small part of how God loves his children.

ACT OF KINDNESS

Spend some time playing with a younger child today.

Extraordinary

The angel said to her, "Do not be afraid, Mary. God is very pleased with you. You will become pregnant and give birth to a son. You must call him Jesus."

LUKE 1:30-31 NIRV

Mary was an ordinary person who got asked to do an extraordinary thing. Something incredible came through one obedient person. There's no doubt Mary was the right one for the job, as the Bible says, she found favor with God, and she was chosen to do one of the biggest acts in our Christian faith!

You may feel ordinary in this life, but you are not. God sees your hard work, your heart, and your ability to do great things for him. God has used many people to achieve his great plan of saving all who are lost. He wants to use you in his heavenly kingdom!

ACT OF KINDNESS

Buy a Christmas gift for someone who doesn't have much.

Born to us

A child has been born for us, a son given to us;
authority rests upon his shoulders; and he is named
Wonderful Counselor, Mighty God,
Everlasting Father, Prince of Peace.

ISAIAH 9:6 NRSV

When someone has a new baby, there is an incredible moment of joy and hope that comes with the sign of new life. This is what was given to us when Jesus was born. He came in a very humble form, but when he arrived, it meant a new beginning was coming for all of us.

The life of Jesus was s huge gift. Through him we can know what God is like, and because of him, we will spend eternity in heaven. As you celebrate Christmas this year, spend some time marveling at what Jesus has done for all people and for all time. Make it your goal to share his gift of life, light, and love with others.

ACT OF KINDNESS

*Create peace by not arguing with
your parents or siblings today.*

Incredible Kindness

God can point to us in all future ages as examples of the incredible wealth of his grace and kindness toward us, as shown in all he has done for us who are united with Christ Jesus.

EPHESIANS 2:7 NLT

God's kindness is what makes it possible for us to be saved from our sin and death. It is not his anger that moves us, but his kindness. There is power in kindness: the kind of power that moves hearts and changes lives. Sometimes people think kindness is weak, but that's not true. Being kind takes a lot of strength.

Look for God's kindness. Don't assume that he is angry with you or that you are too far away from him. His arms are always wide open. No matter how many times you have failed him, he is still merciful and kind.

ACT OF KINDNESS

Leave a nice note on your parents' bed.

A Natural Flow

> He has told you, o man, what is good,
> and what does the LORD require of you.
> But to do justice, and to love kindness,
> and to walk humbly with your God.
>
> MICAH 6:8 ESV

God asks us to seek justice. He wants us to live knowing the difference between right and wrong and to choose to do the right thing. We should love and be kind. We can't do this on our own. We shouldn't even try. When we walk this way, we understand that we are nothing without God. We need his love to be able to do what he has asked.

When we ask, God will help us to be humble in our heart toward others. When people ask questions, we can go to God and ask for his answers instead of giving our own opinions. When we ask him, his compassion and kindness will naturally flow from us.

ACT OF KINDNESS

*Tell a friend or family member
how much you appreciate them.*

Gentle Kindness

> Always be humble and gentle.
> Be patient with each other,
> making allowance for each other's faults
> because of your love.
>
> EPHESIANS 4:2 NLT

Gentleness is found where love and kindness meet. We can ask God for gentleness, and he will answer by giving his opinion on something. God's kindness brings the gentleness we need. It spreads in the heart of a believer, inspiring tenderness toward all.

We can ask the Holy Spirit to train us in gentleness. We ask him to change the way we think so our hearts grow with more compassion. God is steadfast; he doesn't get frustrated with our lack of growth. He helps us grow so we can treat others with his kindness.

ACT OF KINDNESS

Do someone else's dishes.

Faithfully Famous

The Lord is always good and ready to receive you.
He's so loving that it will amaze you—
so kind that it will astound you!
And he is famous for his faithfulness toward all.
Everyone knows our God can be trusted,
for he keeps his promises to every generation!

PSALM 100:5

God is always good. Do you believe that? It is easy for us to look at life and question God's goodness because we only see from our view. But we do know that he is faithful. In fact, he is famous for his faithfulness!

There is no one as faithful as God. We can trust him because he keeps his Word. His kindness and love are amazing. We can trust him always because he is good. Because of this, we can choose to be kind to others even if they are not kind first.

ACT OF KINDNESS

Post encouraging sticky notes around your home.

NO COMPLAINT

When troubles of any kind come your way,
consider it an opportunity for great joy.
For you know that when your faith is tested,
your endurance has a chance to grow.

JAMES 1:2-3 NLT

God has been kind to us. Do we believe it, or do we doubt it? We can probably come up with a long list of things that don't feel like God's kindness. A friend was mean. A family member is sick. A teacher has favorites. When God came to earth as a baby, he was being kind. When he suffered for our sin, he was being kind. When he gave the Holy Spirit to comfort us, he was being kind.

We owe God every breath. Even when we complain, he listens, he cares, and he responds. Don't let bitterness take away what God has done. Remember the truth: God has been kind to you.

ACT OF KINDNESS

Make today a no-complaining day.

A Hopeful Future

"I say this because I know what I am planning for you," says the LORD. "I have good plans for you, not plans to hurt you. I will give you hope and a good future."

JEREMIAH 29:11 NCV

Today is a good chance to look back at your year. What are you proud of? What do you regret? It has been a year of doing simple acts of kindness, and these are exactly the things that will bring the love of Christ to the world around you. Be proud of who you are in Christ and for becoming someone who has chosen to love others.

As you look to the new year, what plans are you making? Don't forget that you might plan your ways, but God knows what is best for you. He has a great future for you. Thank him for every success and failure. Bring him into the next year full of hope for what is to come. May God bless you and keep you.

ACT OF KINDNESS

Allow the kindness of God to settle on your heart and bring you hope for tomorrow.